A ROUND WITH THE TOUR PROS

A ROUND WITH
THE TOUR PROS

STEVE NEWELL

CollinsWillow

An Imprint of HarperCollins*Publishers*

First published in hardback in Great Britain in 2002 by
CollinsWillow an imprint of HarperCollins*Publishers* London

Text © Golf World 2002
Photographs © Allsport and emap 2002

9 8 7 6 5 4 3 2 1

A CIP catalogue record for this book is available
from the British Library

The HarperCollins website address is: www.fireandwater.com

ISBN 0 00 712950 5

Design by 'omedesign (Martin Topping)

Printed and bound in Italy.

CONTENTS

INTRODUCTION

It was during one of our many meetings to discuss Golf World's boldest redesign in nearly 20 years that the editorial team first came up with the idea of pitting one of the magazine's writers against one of the world's best golfers. As far as we were aware it had never been done before in a golf magazine – which, looking back, isn't altogether surprising. Let's not forget tour pros play golf for a living; teasing them out onto a golf course during some precious time off to play against a comparative hacker is a bit like asking you or me to work on a Sunday morning – without pay. In short, not appealing.

Still, if you don't ask, you don't get. We set our sights first on Jesper Parnevik, not only because he was a suitably big name, but also because at that time he had an affiliation with the magazine. His management group IMG put the idea to him and Jesper, being the good man he is, agreed to play even though it wasn't strictly in line with the terms of his contract. I was the lucky guy who got to tee it up against Jesper – a dream assignment that more than lived up to expectations. After the feature was published we received some fantastic feedback from readers. IMG were pleased and so too, we heard, was Jesper. We could not have wished for more.

Charged with enthusiasm and optimism, we bombarded players and managers for more challenge matches. Considering the nature of the request we genuinely believed we'd be fortunate to get more than a couple of games before the series dried up. To our great surprise, and way beyond even our most optimistic hopes, we'd played more than 25 challenge matches against some of the greatest golfers in the world, legends such as Gary Player, Peter Thomson, Ernie Els, Nick Faldo, Ian

Woosnam and many more. Some of the matches took more than a year to arrange, others seemed almost to drop into our laps. We travelled around England, Scotland, Ireland and Wales, and further afield to Monte Carlo, Sweden, Spain, Portugal and the United States.

This book is tangible, glossy proof of what can be achieved through sheer persistence, persuasion and good fortune. It features the pick of the crop, every one a tournament winner, 10 of the 20 a Major champion. As a team of writers we were in the privileged position to obtain rare insight into the game of a top tour pro. With our frantic scribbling of notes and diligent taping of words spoken between shots, we hope we've been able to convey this unique experience and that you benefit as much from reading about these golfers as we did from playing against them.

To the managers who helped arrange these matches we say a big thank you. We couldn't, as they say, have done it without you. We also greatly appreciate the generosity and warm hospitality of the many clubs that allowed us onto their golf courses. But, of course, the most heartfelt thanks must go to the players themselves. For us this wasn't work. It was a pleasure – in some cases virtually a dream come true. For the players, it's fair to say they got the rougher end of the bargain, but without exception they were cooperative, good-humoured and enjoyable to play against. If they gleaned nothing else from the experience, we hope they at least enjoyed a laugh at the odd shot we played ... because some of them were very odd indeed!

Steve Newell
Golf World

ERNIE ELS

I think I now know what it must be like for a team like Barnet FC to pass through the gates of Old Trafford for a cup-tie against the mighty Manchester United. Or maybe to sit on the grid at Silverstone in a Ford and look across to see Michael Schumacher in his scarlet Ferrari. I'm about to take on Ernie Els, three-time World Matchplay champion, on Wentworth's legendary West course, scene of some of his finest moments. You might say my situation is somewhere between No Hope and Bob Hope ... and Bob has just left town!

A formidable opponent if ever there was ... Ernie Els tees off at the first on Wentworth's West Course, a course on which he has won three World Matchplay championships.

HIS SWING LOOKS SO RELAXED AND UNDER CONTROL AND THE BALL SHOOTS OFF THE CLUBFACE LIKE A BULLET

The statistics look ominous. Ernie has knocked it around this gorgeous stretch of Surrey greenbelt in astonishingly low numbers, his birdie count frequently hitting double figures in matches over 30-odd holes. Many of the world's best golfers have been felled under such a barrage. Also, in his four PGA Championship appearances he's a staggering 51 under par for 16 rounds. It's fair to say I could have scoured the planet and not found a tougher man to beat on this course, even with my quota of shots. Wentworth and Ernie are seemingly made for each other.

Still, there is at least one unexpected glimmer of hope – although we're talking very small glimmers. Ernie was pushing weights in the gym two days ago and is experiencing a little muscle stiffness in his arms. As you can see from the pictures accompanying this feature, this doesn't stop him swinging the club sublimely well, but everything's operating at a slightly slower speed than usual. Mind you, even at less-than-full power Ernie's game oozes class in every department.

I notice as the round goes on that his iron shots almost always seem to start between the right edge of the green and the flag itself. It's like a 'corridor' down which the ball travels; then it's just a question of how much draw he wants on the ball to bring it into the flag. These soft-landing draws are his stock shot, although he just as easily works the ball the other way when the situation calls for it.

His long-iron play must be considered one of his strengths. He hits a few awesome long irons off the deck – in particular a piercing 2-iron off the 6th tee – the clubhead barely bruising the manicured Wentworth turf. His swing looks so relaxed and under control – an eye opener for anyone who feels the need to hit their long irons hard – and the ball shoots off the clubface like a bullet. A case of good mechanics and pure timing.

Aside from the great shots, I'm struck by the fact that his bad shots seem hardly ever to do any damage. I've heard it said before by tour pros that being a successful golfer is as much about the terrible shots you don't hit as the great shots you do hit. I'm beginning to see what they mean. To be honest, Ernie doesn't hit many poor shots. But those he does hit are so ... how can I put it? Not that poor. A bad drive for Ernie merely seems to leak a little right, no dramas, perhaps travelling 20 yards shorter than a solid hit. A mistimed iron shot is, if anything, less perceptible. The ball even flies on a nice trajectory, not higher, lower or sideways as it would with you or me.

All of this, I suppose, is coming as no surprise to you. The man has, after all, won two US Opens and umpteen tournaments and held the world number one spot. But what's it really like to

Big Ernie generates phenomenal power from the easiest looking swing – a combination of great technique and superb timing.

ERNIE ON ... ROUGH CHIPS

This is one of the toughest chip shots in the book. The ball is lying in rough with the grass growing away from the target. To make matters worse, this is a downhill lie, too. Any time the grass is like this you've got to treat it like a bunker shot. That's what you can see me demonstrating in this sequence of photographs. Open your stance and the clubface, make a longer swing than you would from a decent lie, and aim to strike a point roughly two inches behind the ball. I feel like I let the weight of the club generate the necessary force through impact. It's almost a lazy action, with a soft grip and a slow pace to the swing. Make sure you keep the clubhead moving through the ball. Do not attempt to strike the ball cleanly with a delicate action. The clubface gets snagged in the grass and the ball travels nowhere. Treat it like a bunker shot, letting the grass cushion the blow in the same way sand does in a splash shot.

**Picture perfect pose –
Ernie reaches the top of
his backswing in great
shape, poised to unleash
another powerful, straight
drive.**

HE HAS THIS ABILITY TO MAINTAIN CONTROL OVER THE DISTANCE THE BALL FLIES FROM ALMOST ANY KIND OF LIE

compete against this sort of golfer? Well, talking
in match terms, I can tell you it feels as if you're
constantly swimming against a strong tide. Even
when there's nothing in it, which there isn't after
ten holes, I get the impression Ernie's on a casual
jog, so to speak, and I'm having to run at full tilt
just to keep up.

On the 11th hole, a pretty tough dogleg par 4,
Ernie finds a toughish lie in the rough, but hits
the green no problem with a tidy 6-iron. Therein
lies another aspect of Ernie's game that is worth
highlighting. He has this ability to maintain
control over the distance the ball flies from almost
any kind of lie. There are a couple of occasions
during our game when Ernie's ball is in what I
consider to be an awkward lie, the rough being
lush and green after June's sunshine and showers,
but he just thumps it out with those big forearms.
I wouldn't say the lie makes no difference,
because it's difficult to spin the ball out of rough,
but he can so obviously create extra force when
required with no loss of control.

On the next hole, the par-5 12th, Ernie fails to
find the green in two but a neat 50-yard pitch to
12 inches produces a gimme birdie. That puts me
two down. That remains the state of play as we
make our way to the 15th tee, where I will be
receiving my final stroke. Ernie doesn't catch his

tee shot flush, but it still splits the fairway, and from there he hits the prettiest-looking iron shot of the day, a pure 5-iron that starts over the right-hand greenside bunker and draws ever so softly in towards the flag. The pitch mark is only inches from the hole, the ball coming to rest seven feet away. His birdie putt looks in all the way, but curls around the back of the cup and stays out. A six-footer for par earns me a desperately needed win.

Even so, I'm still one down with three to play against the three-time World Matchplay champion, and with no shots to come. Oh dear. A bit like trying to get six numbers in the National Lottery, I feel: mathematically possible, yes, but not likely in this lifetime. I figure that even if I make three birdies it probably won't be enough, since the final two holes on the West course are

Ernie's ball striking is astonishingly consistent and even his poor shots are not exactly what you'd call poor.

ERNIE ON ...
PUTTING THOUGHTS

I'm setting up to the ball now with my hands and arms a touch further away from my body than they used to be. It's not a big change, but it's enough to make a difference to how my stroke feels. My hands and arms can swing more freely from here, which means the putter swings more freely too. This helps improve the rhythm of my putting stroke, an important factor that often gets overlooked. From close range, unless there's any sort of break on the putt, I like to work on keeping the face looking at the hole as it travels through impact. That's something you might want to focus on to help improve your holing-out skills.

reachable par 5s and Ernie eats those for breakfast.

We halve the 16th, which does my cause no good at all. I'm now one down with two to play, facing one of the most intimidating drives in golf. Ernie nails his down the middle with draw, but the reverse camber of this fairway sweeps his ball down into the right rough. His second shot finishes in the left rough, some 60 yards short of the pin. As Ernie makes a couple of practice swings I can sense him eyeing a landing area on the green and getting a feel for the length of swing required to produce that amount of carry. The calculations are spot-on. His pitch floats high, lands softly and trickles towards the hole. I'm standing alongside him and to me it looks as if it's going to drop in, but the ball slides past and

ERNIE ON ...
WHETHER TO CHIP OR PUTT

In positions where there's only closely mown fringe grass between the ball and the green, there are two choices: either chip it or putt it. The way I see it, if you want to hole it you've got to chip it. There's a lot that can go wrong between your ball and the green and the only way you can eliminate that risk is by playing a chip. Aim to carry the ball over the fringe and land the ball on the green, guaranteeing the most predictable first bounce.

The technique is simple enough. I stand to the ball as comfortably as I can. My feet are close together, with a slightly open stance, and my hands are just ahead of the ball which is opposite my right heel. My grip is just like any other full shot, although I've choked down on my 9-iron a bit for extra control and taken off my glove for maximum feel. Now I just make a short arm swing, not breaking my wrists too much. The key is to accelerate the club through the ball, keeping the hands ahead of the clubhead. No time to be tentative. Even though this is a short shot, it needs to be played with authority.

This is the simplest way to play these chip shots. With a little practice you shouldn't have any difficulty striking the ball nicely virtually every time. Then it's just a case of getting used to judging distance. That comes with experience. If you really are a bit twitchy with your chip shots, or completely lacking in confidence and satisfied with just getting it anywhere in the general area of the hole, you can putt. But as I say, once you've learned this shot I think you'll be happy to chip.

finishes three inches behind the hole. Ernie just looks at me and smiles.

It really is a treat to observe up close how he plays these 50- to 100-yard shots. His judgement of line and length is superb, the technique simplicity itself. He turns his body, swings his arms and hinges the wrists in perfect harmony to produce a length of backswing that enables him to accelerate smoothly in the downswing. It strikes me as being a positive yet at the same time gentle action, which sounds like a contradiction in terms, but that's the impression the tempo of his pitching swing gives.

Anyway, Ernie's exquisite pitch has closed the door on me and the match is over. Another victory for the big fella around the West course. We play the 18th for fun and Ernie signs off with a score of 71. It's about the worst score he could have shot. The only reason he isn't in the mid-60s is a relatively unfruitful day's work with the putter. I can recall two lip-outs and at least three putts where the ball stopped one roll short of the hole, dead on line. His total of 33 putts is probably about 5 more than his tournament average.

For golfers of Ernie's class that is often the main difference between a good and a great round. That and the fact that in our game he hasn't hit quite so many of his mid-iron shots as close as he might expect, which is just as well since it would have signalled a very early bath for yours truly. As it is, the £20 note that goes from my back pocket into Ernie's seems a small price to pay for as good a day's golf as I could ever wish to have.

Another dent in the Golf World budget, but it's money well spent to see one of the world's great golfers in action.

GARY PLAYER

The time is eight o'clock in the morning. The place, Heathrow departure lounge, gate 26. I'm waiting for the man in black, a diminutive figure at 5ft 9in but a true giant of the game. Gary Player, winner of golf's Grand Slam. This particular rendezvous has taken months to arrange – hardly surprising when you look at the man's punishing globetrotting itinerary (he spends just 30-odd days a year in his own bed) – but the waiting is finally over. Today, in the millionaires' playground that is Monte Carlo, I play against one of the greatest golfers who ever lived.

When the great man speaks, it pays to listen. No golfer playing the game today has as much experience as Gary Player and it makes him fascinating company.

Gary displays the sharp putting skills that helped him win nine Major championships, bettered by only two men in history.

Gary arrives right on time. He is dressed in an immaculate blue blazer, black slacks, black polo shirt and polished black brogues. He is tanned and super-trim, as you would expect of someone who does a thousand sit-ups every day, and has distinguished platinum-coloured streaks in his swept-back dark hair. I can't help thinking he must be the healthiest-looking 66-year-old in the world. Years of looking after himself have paid dividends. People used to laugh at him when he came out on tour eating bananas on the golf course. Now everyone does it. Before Gary I doubt there was a single golfer who went to the gym. Now it's frowned upon if a top golfer does not. Even now he goes to the gym every day. His sit-up regime gives him stomach muscles which are table-top firm.

He has come a long way from the poor boy who started out making a paltry £30 a month as an assistant pro in the early 1950s and who pocketed £100 for winning his first pro tournament in South Africa. A long way indeed. Twelve million miles, in fact, which is his rough estimate as to how far he's travelled in his near 50-year career as a tour pro. Twelve million miles! That's a trip to the moon and back 25 times! 'I reckon I'm the most travelled human being on the planet,' he says. I wouldn't argue with that.

It's a mind-boggling statistic, but totally believable when you realize what Gary Player is like. I have yet to meet a person who has more enthusiasm, such unquenchable get-up-and-go for golf and life. 'I love my life,' he says. 'I love people, I love golf. But it's been a hell of a sacrifice being away from home so much, being away from my children, my wife.' Dedication and hunger have driven him on. 'I don't know whether you're born with it, or whether you cultivate it. All

TWELVE MILLION MILES IS HIS ROUGH ESTIMATE AS TO HOW FAR HE'S TRAVELLED IN HIS NEAR 50-YEAR CAREER AS A TOUR PRO

I know is I've always had it. I always kept trying no matter what. I had great determination to succeed, mainly, I think, because I was poor as a youngster. If you're poor and you struggle you're going to be hungry for success. That hunger has never left me.'

As I discover on several occasions over the next two days, Gary has a special way with people. He greets all well-wishers and admirers with enthusiasm and warmth, as though he's been doing the fame thing for 40-odd minutes rather than 40-odd years. Everyone who comes into contact with Gary seems to walk away with a smile on his or her face. Gary says he loves people. People seem to love him too.

We arrive at Nice airport three hours behind schedule and are then whisked away in a black

SAND PLAY IS ONE OF GARY'S GREAT STRENGTHS. HE TELLS ME THAT IN 1969 HE WENT IN 81 BUNKERS DURING THE SEASON AND AVERAGED GETTING DOWN IN TWO ON 79 OCCASIONS

Mercedes, a professional security driver, appropriately and immaculately dressed in black, at the helm. At the hotel we go our separate ways. Gary turns to me and says, 'Pick me up at ten.' The stage is set.

The morning of our showdown dawns bright, with clear blue sky. The Monte Carlo Golf Club is surprisingly quiet, almost eerily so considering the rich, famous and beautiful people who will be here strutting their stuff in a matter of days for the start of the Monte Carlo Invitational, a sort of Pebble Beach pro am for the European Seniors Tour.

We make our way down to the practice ground. Gary has just got his hands on a new Taylor Made driver and is about as excited as a young boy with a new toy. His eyes light up as he tells me about the amount of extra carry he's getting through the air. Bashing balls to the furthest corner of the range, he can hardly tee them up quick enough. He takes out another of his latest clubs, a Callaway 9-wood. 'It's amazing,' he says. 'I can hit it out of almost any lie and carry it 200 yards and it comes down like a wedge. I could never do that with a 3-iron, not even in my prime.' To prove the point, he treads a ball into the turf and

Gary is the greatest bunker player who ever lived. He threatens the hole from sand like most amateurs do with mid-range putts.

GARY ON ... BUNKER SHOTS

I think the main reason I've always played bunker shots so well is because I spent so much time practising. For the average club golfer the first point I'd make is sand play isn't difficult, as long as you stick to three important fundamentals: the set-up, the quick set in the backswing, and the follow-through. In the set-up you need to open your stance, but you must also open the clubface, which you can do simply by twisting the club clockwise so the face looks to the right of your target. Then form your grip. Do not take your grip and then twist the club, because the face will just return to square at impact. A quick wrist set in the backswing is essential, because it gets the club on a slightly steeper plane which allows you to hit down into the sand behind the ball, with your hands leading the way. Last but not least, you must always follow through with bunker shots. Work on these three principles and the ball will come out every time. That leaves you free to concentrate on developing your feel for distance, which comes through repetition.

GARY ON ... ARNIE AND JACK

The first time I ever saw Arnold play was at the Tam O'Shanter tournament in Chicago. The first time I ever saw Jack play was, I think, at Augusta. They were hitting balls on the range. Both were awfully impressive from day one. Arnold — what a pair of hands. Nicklaus — what a pair of legs. So strong. If you had a combination of Arnold's hands and Jack's legs — wow, what a thought that is. But that's going to happen one day. Some day in the future someone will come along and hit it 50 yards past Tiger. One of the things that made Jack such a superstar, though, was that he could play badly and score well. Let me tell you, Jack could play atrocious golf and shoot 66. During the US PGA at Laurel Valley we were in the dining room one night and he told me he couldn't hit a fairway. So I saw him after the first round and said, 'How many fairways, Jack?' And he said, 'Four.' Do you know what he shot? 66! The next day, I saw him again in the dining room and he held up his hand, indicating that he'd hit five fairways. He'd shot 67! Man, he was special. I really enjoyed playing with Nicklaus. He's also a very fine gentleman. Probably the best loser I ever saw in golf. I mean, it's easy to be a good winner. I've never seen a bad winner in my life. But to be a good loser, that's not so easy.

absolutely flushes it, the ball almost knocking the 200-yard marker sign out of the ground. 'Not even Nicklaus could bring a long-iron shot down from that height,' he remarks.

For the tournament the nines on this course are reversed, so our first hole is the par-5 10th on the scorecard. We are both roughly 60 yards short of the green in two. Playing first, I hit my pitch a little on the thin side but it somehow comes to rest six feet left of the flag. 'Oh no!' Gary cries from across the fairway. 'If I'm going to have to play against that sort of luck I'm in big trouble.' His pitch finishes just outside mine, but he holes from ten feet for an opening birdie. I slot mine to match his birdie, but it's a shot hole so I go one up. 'I'm playing against a crook!' Gary cries.

My tee shot at the next finds a greenside bunker. Gary finds the green. As we get to our balls, Gary says to me, 'I'll swap you.' I do a double take. Gary's ball is on the green, with a putt down the tier to the hole 30 feet away. My ball is in the greenside bunker, about 50 feet from the pin. And he wants to swap me. This is a new twist to matchplay golf I'm happy to embrace. Gary then splashes his ball out of the bunker and across the green for a gimme. I trickle my putt down to four feet and miss. I've been had by the king of matchplay!

Gary still strikes his irons with the venom of a man half his age. It's impressive to watch.

GARY ON ... PUTTING

I've never worked on the same thing for long when it comes to putting. I've chopped and changed all through my career. Back in the early days the greens were so slow that your putting stroke needed to be very wristy, so you gave the ball a firm rap. Otherwise you'd never get it up to the hole. Let me tell you, the surface was nowhere near as good, which made holing putts a lot tougher. That's something no one ever seems to talk about when they compare golfers of different eras. Nowadays the greens we play on are so beautiful, everyone's using a smoother, almost stiff-wristed stroke just to get the ball rolling. Forty years ago there wasn't one stiff-wristed putter, now there isn't a single wristy putter.

Sand play is one of Gary's great strengths. He tells me that in 1969 he went in 81 bunkers during the course of a season and averaged getting down in two on 79 occasions. He hasn't lost his touch either. Occasionally when we finish a hole he throws a few balls in the nearest bunker and hops in with his sand-wedge. He hits bunker shots for fun. He nominates each shot as he's standing over the ball. 'Low with spin,' he'll say. 'High with a soft landing.' Each one crafted perfectly to order. Gary threatens the hole from sand like the rest of us do with mid-range putts.

Within the first three or four holes I must say I'm surprised how far he hits the ball off the tee. He is unfeasibly flexible for a man of his age, a shining example of what keeping fit does for you. His swing is long and flowing and he really gives it everything through the hitting area. The man's had 24 holes-in-one and hits his iron shots with venom, taking massive divots with his short irons.

On our sixth hole a purely-struck 7-iron sees the ball keep low into the breeze and finish three feet away, securing Gary's third birdie of the day. On the 11th he hits another good drive, which unluckily for him finishes on a severe upslope in the fairway, some 200 yards short of the green. He rises to the challenge by hitting the shot of the day, a three-quarter punched 3-wood that starts left and fades right into the heart of the green. 'The yardage said it was a 3-iron, but my instinct said if I hit a 3-iron I'll be 30 yards short. So I took a 3-wood, aimed left, took an easy swing and cut it in. That's what I mean when I say to people that being a great player has nothing to do with having the perfect swing. There's much more to it than that.' However, Gary now has a wickedly quick putt down a slippery slope and I feel he will do well to get down in two. His first putt finishes five feet away. Anxious not to let me off the hook, he concentrates harder than on any other putt so far and knocks it straight into the heart. It doesn't matter what the stakes are, Gary loves competing.

I feel I'm fighting a losing battle, and on the 14th I find myself in a predicament that can only be

GARY HAS JUST GOT HIS HANDS ON A NEW TAYLOR MADE DRIVER
AND IS ABOUT AS EXCITED AS A YOUNG BOY WITH A NEW TOY

Handing over cash to fantastically wealthy people is something you grow accustomed to when taking on the greats of the game.

described as dire: three down with four to play against a man who won five World Matchplay Championships. The 15th is make-or-break time. Gary hits his second shot to 15 feet but runs his birdie putt 3 feet past the hole. Given the state of the match I have to make him hole out, not really thinking for a second that he'll miss. Gary does a lot of work for charity, but the 'Steve Newell Fund for Lost Causes' is not on his long list of beneficiaries. He raps the ball into the back of the hole and we shake hands.

As we walk off the green Gary smiles at me and holds open his wallet, inviting me to slot the 100-franc note into it. If there's one thing I've grown accustomed to in this series of matches it's handing over cash to fantastically wealthy people.

Behind the 18th green, our super-cool, man-in-black driver is waiting to whisk us away, back down the mountain. Gary seems positively spritely and tells me that he's off to the gym back at his hotel.

I meet him there to see him in action. He turns up in gym gear – all black, naturally. I ask him if he enjoys training. 'I enjoy the results it gives me,' he responds, 'but if there was a pill I could take which would achieve the same results I'd do that instead.'

Shortcuts have never been Gary's style, though. He's travelled, trained and tried harder than any other golfer and it's impossible to be anything other than massively impressed by what he's achieved. Only two men in history have won more majors than him. And let's not ignore the fact that he had to beat the likes of Nicklaus, Palmer, Watson and Trevino when they were all at the height of their powers.

'I'm still hungry,' he says to me as we say goodbye. 'I want to be the first man to win tournaments in six different decades in America. That would be a great achievement. But the standard of play is so high now. If I do it, I don't think it'll ever be matched. I mean, you've got to live that long for a start!'

HELEN ALFREDSSON

In Irish folklore, 'banshees' are female fairies who announce their presence by shrieking and wailing under the windows of a house when one of its occupants is awaiting death.

Helen Alfredsson's bubbly personality and chatty nature are deceptive, behind the friendly face is a steely competitor.

'Hello, are you ready to play?' Helen shouts up at a window of the clubhouse at Royal Porthcawl.

Alfredsson is a female fairy. She also has a reputation for being one of the toughest matchplayers in the game. Once she gets her teeth into an opponent, she just doesn't let go – like a Jack Russell with very, very long legs. She is so unlike the Swedish stereotype epitomized by Bjorn Borg and Annika Sorenstam it is frightening. The 36-year-old Swede makes Jesper Parnevik look boring. She had anorexia when she was young, did a stint as a model, flew with the Blue Angels, and is one of the most outspoken and candid players in the professional game. Not for Helen the life of the unflappable athlete whose expression never changes whether she's made a birdie or a bogey. Instead, she wears her emotions on both sleeves; but then what would you expect from someone who shares a birthday (9 April) with Seve Ballesteros?

In her Solheim Cup match at Loch Lomond in 2000 (when she played in the second morning's fourball matches with Alison Nicholas against Inkster and Steinhauer) she got so carried away it was actually quite frightening to watch. Her eyes bulged, and she was so focused she made the fiery Dottie Pepper look like a cuddly pussycat. The end

result was that, despite coming into the match playing poorly, she made eight birdies and carried Nicholas to a 3&2 victory.

As we stroll down the 2nd fairway looking across the Bristol Channel in glorious sunshine, Helen is in a less intense mood. That, however, doesn't mean for a moment she's quiet, because she's seldom quiet.

'You know, it has taken the Americans over a year to recover from what happened in the Solheim Cup at Loch Lomond,' she observes. 'I have talked to them all now, because we all play on the same tour, but it took a year. There was a lot of hostility this time around with what happened to Annika, and then Dottie gets up and says, "If it wasn't for the LPGA Tour then all the European players would be packing groceries." Someone asked me what I thought about that comment. I just wanted to know whether she wanted plastic or paper.'

When Helen was only 18, she went to Paris, because she wanted to try a career as a model. 'When I was young I was overweight and ugly. Suddenly, I lost a lot of weight and someone suggested I do it. So I did.'

She is impulsive by nature. She once fired a caddie on the 6th hole of a US Open. At university in San Diego, she fell in love with the men's soccer coach, Leo Cuellar, despite the fact that falling in love with members of the teaching staff was not the done thing. 'It was very illegal,' she has said. 'Isn't love more fun that way?'

'I have decided that it doesn't matter if I try not to get into trouble,' she says after I have put myself in deep trouble off the 3rd tee. 'I'm the sort of person who is still going to get into trouble without even trying. With some people that's just the way it is.'

Cuellar played football for Mexico, but his 15-year affair with Helen Alfredsson ended last year. She's now dating an ice hockey player called Kent. They met at a mutual friend's wedding. What is it about sports stars?

'He's a golf nut,' she says. 'In fact, he's coming here, so you can meet him. Golf takes such a long time to play, it helps if your partner plays. I think that is quite important. Look at Antonio Garrido and Samantha Head. Golf takes so long, that's why there are so many divorces.'

At that moment Helen's mobile phone rings. It's Kent. He has landed at Stansted and is on his way to Porthcawl.

'NO WONDER YOU FIND GOLF SO EXCITING,' SAYS ALFIE. 'YOU NEVER KNOW WHERE YOU'RE GOING TO HIT IT NEXT.'

Helen is an exciting golfer to watch – her naturally flamboyant character is reflected in the cavalier approach of her golf game (above).

Helen drives the ball long and straight, which is only one of the reasons I struggle to stay in touch (left).

SHE HAD ANOREXIA WHEN SHE WAS YOUNG, DID A STINT AS A MODEL, FLEW WITH THE BLUE ANGELS, AND IS ONE OF THE MOST CANDID PLAYERS IN THE PROFESSIONAL GAME

'He says he's at junction 29 on the M25,' Helen shouts.

'Shouldn't he be going the other way?' I wonder.

After we have got Kent back on track, Helen holes a monster putt on the 9th green as if to celebrate, and goes two up.

One of the most legendary stories about Helen Alfredsson concerns her appearance at the Tour School in America in 1990. At great expense, she flew out to the States to try her hand on a different continent and arrived at the course on which the tournament was due to be played. As she was practising on the putting green, a whisper went round that someone had forgotten to register. It was, of course, H. Alfredsson. Without playing a single shot, she had to pack up her bags and fly all the way back to Britain – where she promptly went and won the British Open.

'That's just typical me,' she says. 'I don't think I'm really an airhead, it's just there's a lot of things going on in my head and I'm just not that organized. I always had a messy room as a child; in fact, even now I leave things lying around everywhere. Life seems to move so fast and yet it gets boring if you have every second of your life planned. I have found that the most precious things in life often happen spontaneously.'

As we wait on the 11th tee (a lovely little par 3 over a valley to a green surrounded by bunkers) I'm intrigued to find out what goes on inside Alfie's head just before she hits a shot.

'Do you have any special swing thoughts at present?' I ask.

'You know, sometimes it's better to have 50,000 swing thoughts rather than one.' She notices I'm looking a touch confused. 'My point is, the golf swing only takes two seconds. If you have 50,000 swing thoughts then, that way, you don't really have any.'

Helen lives for the minute and scarcely looks much further ahead in life than the ball in front of her.

I step up to the tee.

'Stand back!' Alfie shouts as I'm over the ball, waving at a couple of locals who have come to watch. What gamesmanship! Wilting by the second and bemused by her logic, I scuff one into a particularly deep pot bunker on the right of the green.

'No wonder you find golf so exciting,' says Alfie. 'You never know where you're going to hit it next.'

Three down.

Helen's mobile rings again.

'Kent says he's on the M3,' she shouts across the 12th fairway. 'Is he on the right road?' I calmly explain he is on the right road if he wants to go to Basingstoke, Winchester or Southampton, but for Royal Porthcawl, the M4 is preferable. 'M4, Kent. You've got to get on the M4.'

Although she is thrashing me, Helen Alfredsson is one of the world's great under-achievers. When she burst onto the professional scene in the late 1980s, she very soon became Rookie of the Year on both sides of the Atlantic and won the British Open. People ran out of adjectives to describe her natural ability. She won her only major in 1993, at the Nabisco Dinah Shore, and three months later found herself leading the US Open going into the final round. On the Sunday morning she received a mysterious wake-up call at 4.30. Of course, she couldn't get back to sleep and eventually got to the course exhausted. Then there was an hour's delay for rain. 'My mind was crazy by the time I got out there,' she recalls. No surprise, then, that she shot a final-round 74.

By the time we reach the 14th green I'm struggling to keep the match going, and, in fact, three-putt to lose 5&4.

'Oh well,' Helen says by way of commiseration, 'win or lose, there's always booze.'

We play the last four holes just for the hell of it and I make one last discovery. The 36-year-old Swede has no time for this current trend for political correctness.

'It makes me sick,' she says. 'I'd rather be called a "girl" than a "woman" any day of my life. When you become a woman, you are on the way out. In America, you wouldn't believe how bad it gets. And the law over there is ridiculous. Do you remember that woman who got burnt by the coffee? That's exactly the sort of woman who would complain if the coffee was too cold for her.'

I ask her if she has mellowed with age.

'No, I don't think so,' she answers. 'I'm still a

HELEN ON ... PUTTING: LOOK AT THE LINE, NOT AT THE CUP

On breaking putts a lot of amateurs tend to look at the cup rather than the line they are putting to. The absolute crucial thing when putting is you have to line up properly. That way, you have given yourself a line in your head. Where you are aiming is even more important on the green than on longer shots, because on longer shots you have time to compensate. So, if you have a putt which breaks six feet from right to left, you must look at the spot on the green six feet right of the cup, not at the hole. Then you can just hit the putt at that spot and let the break take effect. It's a much better system.

kid in a lot of ways. When you've been through as many ups and downs as I have, you just really crave some peace and quiet – nothing extravagant. When I was younger, I loved to see my picture and name in the papers, but I've done that. Now, little things like a glass of wine with friends make me happy.'

Children?

'I love other people's but I think if I was meant to have kids I would probably have had them by now.'

As a postscript, I would just like to put on record that before our match, Helen Alfredsson had not won a tournament for three years. Twenty-four hours after it, she teed it up in the WPGA Championship of Europe and beat a star-studded field with some ease. I am adamant the two events are not unconnected. If there are any tour pros out there going through a bad patch, I am open to offers.

Kent never arrived. Presumably caught in traffic somewhere in the Home Counties ...

IAN POULTER

As recently as 1999, Ian Poulter was selling hotdogs as assistant pro at Leighton Buzzard Golf Club. On a gloomy November day a few years later, Ian returns to his home club as Italian Open champion and the European Tour's Rookie of the Year. Attached to such a moniker are great expectations. Previous winners include the likes of Tony Jacklin, Sam Torrance, Nick Faldo, Sandy Lyle, José María Olázabal, Colin Montgomerie and Sergio Garcia. You would think this might weigh heavy on a man's mind. Not Ian Poulter's. Indeed, I get the distinct impression Ian is not in the least bit fazed. 'When I was young Nick Faldo, who grew up not far from my home, was one of my inspirations so it's just great to follow in his footsteps,' he says. Rookie of the Year is just another stepping stone down the road he obviously sees quite clearly in front of him, a road paved with the gold that great golf brings.

My first impressions of Ian's golf game are all positive. He's one of the quickest players I've ever seen. Once he's addressed the ball he has a couple of brisk waggles, a final look at the target, then bang! He hits it. Even during tournaments he likes to play by instinct, basically to go with the flow and not get bogged down. 'I don't hang around, not ever,' he confirms. 'I think you can stand there too long and start thinking about too much. Obviously I think you've got to picture in your mind the shot you want to play, but once you're over the ball just get on with it.' Not only

does he play his golf with a refreshing lack of lingering, he soon forgets about bad shots. 'To be honest, I don't think about them at all. As far as I'm concerned a bad shot is a bad shot, that's all. You've just got to get rid of it and try to focus on something positive for the next shot. I'm a positive person anyway, so that's the way I try to be on the golf course.'

He's a fantastic driver of the ball, a powerful striker and eager to give it a rip irrespective of the space available. As his coach Lee Scarbrow said to me before we went out, 'Ian's strongest

Into the perfect slot at the top, Ian has worked hard on getting into this position and not over-swinging.

THE LOWDOWN ON IAN

When Ian left school he went to work for Lee Scarbrow in the pro shop at Leighton Buzzard Golf Club in Bedfordshire. Lee has always been a great believer in Ian's ability, and when he first secured his card for the Challenge Tour Lee basically said to him, 'Enough is enough, just go out there and play.' He's understandably thrilled with how Ian has progressed. 'Ian's strongest attribute, no question, is his strength of mind. If you've got someone with that mental toughness then you can tidy up the rough edges and you'll have a class act on your hands. And that's what the boy is. He will get better and better.'

HE'S A FANTASTIC DRIVER OF THE BALL, A POWERFUL STRIKER AND EAGER TO GIVE IT A RIP IRRESPECTIVE OF THE SPACE AVAILABLE

attribute, no question, is his strength of mind.' Ian himself says, 'I'm a very aggressive player. If a shot's on, then I'll have a go at it. I don't like laying up.'

This confidence has been more than backed up by his actions since turning pro. The very first event Ian played in as a professional, at the age of 19, was an Eastern Counties two-round tournament. Having birdied the 15th in his first round Ian thought he would quickly run through his scorecard, at which point he realized he was

eight under par. 'I thought to myself, "Holy shit!" I bogeyed two of the last three, but I still finished six under, which at the time I thought was okay. I followed that up with another 66 the next day and won the tournament in a record score. The £1,500 first prize seemed like a lot at the time.'

Clearly, Ian is the sort of person who builds on success rather than rests on his laurels. He's managed to win a tournament every year since turning pro, gradually improving and progressing through the various mini-tours until in 1999 he qualified for the Challenge Tour, which stood him in good stead for a year with the big boys. 'Playing four rounds every week is great practice. I think if I'd got my card for the main tour in 1999 I wouldn't really have been ready. But I

Through the ball Ian is as good as anyone. It's his aggressive ball-striking that makes him one of the most exciting young players in Europe.

IAN ON ... THE DRAMA OF OPEN QUALIFYING IN 2000

I bogeyed the last hole in final qualifying at Ladybank to fall back into a five-way play-off for three spots. I went to the practice ground and started hitting 7-irons, because I knew the first play-off hole was the par-3 10th, which I guessed would be a 7-iron. Anyway, I holed two 7-irons out of ten balls. I thought, 'I'm fine now.' Walking to the tee, though, I found I was really nervous, for the first time ever really. Two guys hit their tee shots before me. I was third to play, and I hit the perfect 7-iron. I even shouted 'Get in!' when the ball was in the air. The ball took one bounce, checked and horseshoed round the hole to about six inches. We were walking up to the green and I was thinking, 'Job done.' It was the most enjoyable short putt I'd ever had.

At the Open I got a nightmare starting time: four o'clock in the afternoon. It took us three hours to play the front nine. It was virtually dark when we got to the 16th. After I'd hit my drive on the Road Hole I got to my ball and couldn't see the flag. On the last it was ridiculous. It was so dark I left my first putt six feet short, but holed that for a 74, which wasn't awful in the circumstances. I went out the next day and played great for a 69 to make the cut. I really wanted to have that walk up the 18th on Sunday afternoon, at whatever time. I couldn't have picked a better first Open than St Andrews.

gained a lot of experience from the Challenge Tour and I felt comfortable coming out on tour earlier this year.'

It showed. As early as midway through his rookie season Ian had guaranteed his tour card for the following year. Neither he nor his coach was satisfied, though. They had predicted better things, and better things arrived in the shape of a first tournament win at the Italian Open. I find it fascinating listening to Ian's thoughts on this hugely significant breakthrough. It's intriguing to know what goes through a player's mind in that situation, especially when the player has never been there before.

'I was three shots clear going into the last round, which I felt was a comfy lead. But it's hard to go out there and start firing at flags, because they're tucked away on the last day and if you miss the green on the wrong side those mistakes cost you shots and I didn't want to make any mistakes. By the 12th hole, though, I found myself two shots behind Gordon Brand Jr. That kicked me into gear. I holed a massive putt on the 14th, which really got me fired up. I made par on the next. Then I had two par 5s in a row and I knew I had to do something. I hit a great drive off 15 and hit a 3-iron to 15 feet. I missed my eagle putt, but made birdie. On the next I made a par. Then on the 17th I knew I had a great chance, because the previous year I'd played a Challenge Tour event on the same course and I remembered making a birdie on that hole. That was something positive to think of. I didn't see any reason why I shouldn't make another birdie. And I did. I was extremely pumped up by then.

'As I was walking to the 18th tee I heard a groan from the gallery up ahead, which I figured meant Brand had made a bogey. At that point it dawned on me that I had to make a four to win. I hit a great drive and the second shot was slightly uphill to a blind green. I hit a 6-iron just where I wanted to, 30 feet left of the pin, which was the safest place to hit it. I was putting well, so I didn't expect to three-putt. I rolled it up to three inches. It felt amazing, awesome. It was a massive adrenalin rush, something I want to get used to.'

Ian got to experience the same feeling the following year, when he notched up his second tournament win and put himself in the frame for a

Ian's tidy short game is at least a match for his exciting long game.

Mental strength is perhaps Ian's strongest suit. When the gun goes his mind is on the job 100 per cent and pressure doesn't faze him.

IAN ON ... LEARNING FROM LANGER'S MASTERFUL COURSE MANAGEMENT

In my first year on tour I feel like I've learned a lot from watching more experienced players. I played with Bernhard Langer in the last round at the B&H and it was fantastic to be able to play with someone like that. I actually played very well on the day, but it was great to watch the way he got it round the golf course. He's renowned as one of the best thinkers out there and his course management is absolutely superb. If ever he hit it into trouble, he'd just play the right shot and put it back into play, basically in a position where he wouldn't make another mistake. You try to pick up on those things and learn from them yourself. I mean, I like to think I don't have any weaknesses, but I suppose if I were to put my finger on one it would be a slight tendency to be overly aggressive at the wrong time. Average players can learn a lot from that too. They make mistake after mistake, which ends up being a total disaster. Players like Langer, after they've hit a bad shot if they've got to take a five they'll take a five. But they won't make it a six or a seven.

ON A GLOOMY NOVEMBER DAY IAN RETURNS TO HIS HOME CLUB AS ITALIAN OPEN CHAMPION AND THE EUROPEAN TOUR'S ROOKIE OF THE YEAR

IAN POULTER IS FULL OF THE JOYS OF SUCCESS, A REAL LIVEWIRE WITH A GREAT PERSONALITY. HE'S CONFIDENT, AND NOT AFRAID TO SAY SO

IAN ON ...
PRACTISING FOR A REASON

If you're just beating balls for the sake of it, you might as well stop. If you can get into the habit of working on something, where you think on every shot, that's what I call a good practice session. That's the way every golfer should practise, whatever the level of ability. Personally, I can practise like that for three or four hours and the time just flies. It's one of the things I've enjoyed in my first year on tour, with the practice facilities being so good. I've probably been a bit lazy in the past, but things are changing and I'm practising a lot harder. I think when you get to this level you've got to put in the work.

IAN ON ...
HIS KEY SWING THOUGHTS

I'm always trying to keep it a bit short in the backswing because I've always had a tendency to overswing a little bit. So that's what we've been working on for a while now, shortening the backswing and keeping it a bit more solid. There's less room for error that way. I'm also trying to work on turning the club more around my body on the way back, because halfway into the backswing I've had a tendency to lift the club up a bit. There are just a few little things, really. I've been trying to weaken my left-hand grip a bit too. I tended to re-grip the club while I was over the ball, and it would get a bit too strong.

Ryder Cup spot – a dream that goes all the way back to boyhood. Ian took up golf at the age of five when his dad gave him a cut-down 3-wood. He and his older brother, who today is also a golf professional, soon started playing golf together at Stevenage. Their sibling rivalry spurred each other on. Each tried desperately to beat the other. For both of them there was only ever going to be one job when they grew up. 'I had it in my mind that I always wanted to be a golf pro,' Ian says, 'so as soon as I got my handicap down to below four, which was the required level, I turned pro straight away. The sooner I turned pro the better as far as I was concerned. I didn't particularly want to play amateur golf at the top level.'

Anyway, back to our game. In typical fashion, Ian has completely ignored the fact that the 8th is a dogleg and simply murdered his drive, launching the ball over the corner and into perfect position leaving him just an easy wedge to the green. He also reduces the tough 465-yard 12th to a drive and a flick with a 9-iron for an easy birdie, then birdies the next two. He's on a roll, and we're coming to crunch time in the match. During a tournament, this is the part of the round Ian relishes. He loves to be in the thick of it and freely admits to wanting to show what he can do in front of the cameras. 'I like to play when the adrenalin is high,' he says. 'There's no better feeling. That's when I enjoy my golf more, no question. And it's when I play my best too.'

At 24 years of age Ian Poulter is full of the joys of success, a real livewire with a great personality. He's confident, and not afraid to say so. He so obviously enjoys what he does. I think his whole approach to the game and the way he plays is a breath of fresh air. One of his main sponsors for his first year on tour was *The Sun* newspaper; they must have been delighted with the way things went. Ian was equally pleased with the arrangement. 'I borrowed a Ferrari for the week, had a photo shoot with a page-three girl, then when I got through to the Open the paper ran a daily "Ian's diary" which was great publicity for me. Certainly more people knew who I was than if I hadn't done it.' I think even more people will know about Ian Poulter in years to come.

With superb all-round skills and the right mental approach, Ian is looking at a great future in the game.

You should listen when a former Masters champion gives you the line of a putt.

IAN WOOSNAM

Think of Ian Woosnam hitting a shot. Any shot will do. What do you see? The pronounced waggle of the club as he settles over the ball? The oh-so-simple swing? The ripping drives and punchy iron shots? Probably all of these things. Over the years Woosie's mannerisms have become so distinctive that a crystal-clear image springs to mind. You may even conjure a mental picture of his purposeful stride between shots. When playing well, he looks as if he can't wait to get to his ball and give it another thump.

Woburn's narrow, tree-lined fairways inevitably call for some creative shot making, a talent that Woosie has in abundance.

Woosie has always been the sort of golfer who makes a lasting impression. I have seen him hit hundreds of shots on TV and witnessed many of his finest hours – the Masters win in 1991, thrilling Ryder Cup matches, titanic battles in the World Matchplay and countless tour victories. When I took up golf in my teens, he was one of the men to watch. He's remained so ever since.

Lately, though, things have changed a bit. During the late 1990s Woosie wasn't quite his old self. He's not over the hill, but, as with the other members of Europe's big five (Seve Ballesteros, Sandy Lyle, Bernhard Langer and Nick Faldo), Father Time is tugging at his cashmere sleeve and trying to stop him being great again. He's had back problems too,

which have inevitably affected his form. Even more painfully, perhaps, he's had so much grief on the greens that he resorted to dabbling with the broomhandle putter – although that's since looked like being a smart decision, because he has been putting really well. The question is, how strong is Woosie's desire to recapture former glories?

Within half an hour of teeing off in this pro am the day before the British Masters, I can see there is very little cause for concern. We start at Woburn's par-5 10th, and he holes a 20-footer for birdie. Then he smacks a 5-iron to 10 feet on the par-3 11th and slots that putt too. Two under after two will do nicely.

This opening blast is in stark contrast to the shaky start made by his humble playing partners today. Woosie tries to put us all at ease with some tales of his own 1st-tee nerves, although he's talking about a far bigger stage and an audience numbered in their millions rather than the few stragglers trailing us down the 3rd fairway. 'When you play in a Ryder Cup the butterflies are unbelievable,' he says. 'The first time at PGA National in 1983 I was playing with Sam

> 'WHEN YOU PLAY IN A RYDER CUP THE BUTTERFLIES ARE UNBELIEVABLE. THE FIRST TIME IN 1983 I WAS PLAYING WITH SAM TORRANCE, AND I FELT SO BAD, I TOLD HIM I WAS GOING TO BE SICK'

Torrance, and I felt so bad I told him I was going off into the trees to be sick. He said, "Don't worry, I'll look after you for the first few holes until you get going." As it turned out, I hardly saw him for the first few holes. I was virtually playing by myself. He was out of bounds, then he was in the water, and I was thinking, "Thanks a lot, Sam." But I think I started birdie, par, birdie. That was the best possible start, and it settled me down pretty quickly.'

I have to confess that draining long putts is the last thing I expected from Woosie today. I thought he was still a bit shaky with the short stick. But I'm wrong. On greens that are pretty slippery, his putting looks smooth throughout the round – confident from medium range and solid from closer in. On the 18th green I remark on how impressed I am with his stroke. 'Let's see how I twitch them tomorrow,' he says, and smiles, suggesting it might

Getting up-close and personal to watch a boyhood hero hitting shots is an experience to savour at every opportunity.

WOOSIE ON ...
PUNCHY SHORT-IRON PLAY

Many amateurs struggle to hit pitch shots in the 60- to 90-yard range. The key to these in-between shots is the length of your backswing. Too long, and you have to decelerate into impact to avoid hitting the ball too far. That gives you a really inconsistent strike. You hit some heavy, some thin. Even the ones you hit well probably miss the green over the back. Instead, you need to make what feels like a shorter backswing, so you can accelerate the club into impact. This positive move through the ball tends to produce a descending blow and gives you crisper contact.

WOOSIE IS THE ANTITHESIS OF A MECHANICAL GOLFER, AND
REALLY DOES MAKE SWATTING A GOLF BALL LOOK VERY EASY

Woosie's iron play is a joy to watch, it seems to come as naturally to him as throwing a ball, and the trajectory is awesome.

be a different story under pressure when he tees it up in the tournament proper.

Many a true word is spoken in jest, and poor putting seems the only conceivable reason for his recent slide down Europe's money list. There certainly doesn't seem much wrong with his ball striking. This is the Woosie I remember of old. His sturdy physique and powerful arms combine to give the ball a pretty solid wallop. The narrow, tree-lined fairways of Woburn's Duke's Course are a bit too claustrophobic for him to give the driver the full treatment, but that doesn't matter much. As Ian says, 'There's often no point hitting a driver here.' Certainly not when you hit a Callaway steel-headed 3-wood 275 yards without a thought. Very impressive. He even nudges 300 yards on a couple of occasions.

Woosie's irons are still the heart of his game, though. The stunning 2-iron he hit from behind trees on the 13th in the 1991 Masters, on his charge to victory, remains one of the greatest televised shots ever. I'll never forget the ball fizzing off into the distance with a sublime draw, eventually coming to rest on the green some 220 yards away. Nothing much has changed. His rounded swing still seems made for hitting shots like this. It looks like 'two turns and a swish' – which might seem a simplistic description, but that's the beauty of Woosie's game. He's the antithesis of a mechanical golfer and really does make the job of swatting a golf ball look very easy.

Essentially, his technique hasn't changed in 20 years, but a few bad habits have crept in. That's why he recently called in high-profile coach Pete

WOOSIE ON ... THE FLOP SHOT OVER THE BUNKER

Mentally this is a tough shot for some amateurs, but basically you have to play it like a bunker shot. The same rules apply. Open your stance, lay the clubface open and make a smooth swing, much longer than you would from the same distance on a good lie. Don't think about striking the ball cleanly. Just slide the club through the grass under the ball, just as you do through sand in a bunker, and keep your nerve. The problems start when you don't trust yourself, and you decelerate into impact or have a dig at the ball. Play a few practice shots from rough around the putting green so that you're not terrified when you face the same shot on the golf course.

Cowen, who looks after a stable of European tour stars including the likes of Lee Westwood, Thomas Bjorn and Darren Clarke, to administer some fine-tuning. 'I've been working with Pete since the Open in 1999,' Woosie explains. 'He knows my game inside out, and we've changed my swing to try to revive my old draw. I'm starting to strike the ball pretty solidly again, and I've even gained a few yards. The trouble is, I'm still scared to aim down the right because I've hit so many blocks over the last couple of years. But it's getting there.'

I can tell his game is at that 'nearly but not quite' stage. The mental scars caused by a lack of trust in his swing manifest themselves in the occasional wayward drive, on holes where I suspect he would hit a long iron or 3-wood in tournament play. But on the whole his golf looks strong – although sadly not strong enough to shoulder three erratic partners whose games don't so much knit together as fall apart at the seams. Each of us has his moments, when the stroke index transforms a hard working par into red figures. But fleeting moments are not enough. To win a pro am the amateurs need to be using all their shots, knocking in the occasional long putt and generally not relying on the pro to secure all the birdies. Unsurprisingly, we finish well down the pecking order.

Nevertheless, my pro-am debut has been a fruitful experience in other ways. First off, it makes me appreciate the high tolerance levels these top players must have. Don't get me wrong, I'm not saying that playing a pro-am round every week is such a bad deal. Cleaning toilets it is not. But there are times when the pro needs the patience of a particularly patient saint. They encourage shots you feel sure they'd rather turn up their noses at. 'Big bounce!' Woosie says as I dunch a wedge from 80 yards. 'Kick left!' as a pitiful drive heads for the trees. I can't help thinking they must get sick of talking to shots that in all honesty deserve the silent treatment.

I come away with renewed faith in a teenage hero. Woosie is as impressive to watch up close as he is on the small screen. I can see how and why he has amassed 43 professional tournament wins worldwide. There's a fine line, however, between adding to those wins and merely trundling along in mid-field with occasional top-ten finishes. Sadly, at the moment Woosie is the wrong side of that line. He might make it back to the other side, though. The old fighting spirit hasn't left him yet.

WOOSIE ON ... SWING TROUBLE

When I was playing well I'd hit the ball as late as I liked, almost holding it off. Then if I wanted to hit a big draw, I'd just let it go a bit earlier. Having that one shape of shot to rely on took one side of the golf course out of play, which was great. But since I've not been playing great, I've just been aiming down the middle and not really knowing if the ball is going to go left or right. That's no way to play. Pete Cowen and I have been working to get my draw back. Over the years my hands have been getting steadily higher at impact than they were at address. Now I'm trying to keep my hands much lower through the ball, which gets more penetration on my shots. I'm also trying to keep my body down and clear my left side when I come in to the ball. It means I'm turning through the ball much better and I can release the club, instead of coming up out of the shot. Lately I've noticed I can go out and hit the ball well straight away, whereas before I'd have had to hit 30 balls just to get my rhythm. That obviously makes a big difference.

JESPER PARNEVIK

What really happens when a club golfer comes up against one of the best players in the world? Is the gulf in ability so ridiculously wide that it makes a mockery of feeble stroke allowances? Do these guys really play golf from another planet? I'm about to find out.

Lean and tanned, Jesper looks every bit the international golfing superstar.

Jesper pictures every shot very clearly in his mind's eye. He never hits a shot until he's 100 per cent ready.

It's 9.30 a.m. at sunny Wentworth and my long-awaited game with Jesper Parnevik is just 15 minutes away. There's no sign of the man, though, which is worrying. I look at my watch one more time. Just ten minutes to go. At least I'm looking the part: the Masters polo shirt, my best golf shoes – I feel I'm ready for anything. But when Jesper arrives looking tanned, lean and healthier than just about anyone I've ever met, I suddenly realize that only a ten-month rain check and a sabbatical to work on my game will make me even close to ready. If we're talking comfort zones, which I am, you could say I'm way out of one.

On the tee, Jesper loosens up with an unfeasibly heavy golf club weighted with lead, which seems like a good idea. I figure that after a few swings of that, even my unwilling muscles will be stretched into shape. It backfires. My driver suddenly feels as light as a feather, and although Jesper's offer to give me the honour is a generous gesture (he probably thought the poor chap might as well have one chance to tee off first), I can't say I feel

JESPER ON ... FREEING YOUR MIND OVER THE BALL

A lot of bad shots are caused because you got scared of another shot and over-compensate. Say you've hit two hooks on consecutive tees and you come to a hole with trouble down the left. In the downswing I bet you'll be thinking, 'Please God, don't hit it left', and then you make a bad swing and the ball goes right. You get scared of it. You've got to let yourself do what you can do on the practice ground. Decide on a shot and commit yourself 100 per cent to that. Then free your mind and away you go. If you can honestly say to yourself 'I didn't have any doubt in my swing there, I just let it rip', that's great. Even if the shot doesn't come off, you've done all you can do. Don't let your mind ruin your swing. Those mental errors are the ones that hurt the most.

comfortable. Indeed, strangely enough, I don't think I've ever felt so self-conscious. I wasn't expecting that. I don't usually even think about what I look like at address. But suddenly I do. As I go through the usual rigmarole that passes for my pre-shot routine and settle over the ball, I sense that Jesper's trained eye is scrutinizing my grip, my posture, my every move. Just in those few seconds I have time to ponder the disturbing possibility that he may have spotted a catalogue of faults.

My first swing is at least mercifully quick, but it isn't good. The ball enjoys a brief look down the fairway before taking on the shape of a snap-hook. I think I feel comforted by a remark from Jesper's caddie: 'And you looked so good before you hit it.' But then again, perhaps not.

Jesper's demeanour is so self-assured. Granted, that's not surprising, but even so I'm struck by how comfortable he looks over the ball, how purposefully he waggles the club. I notice that, considering the size of his driver, the ball is teed remarkably low. His brisk swing is familiar, but I'm not quite prepared for the blistering speed through impact.

JESPER ON ... LEARNING FROM OTHERS

Even at my level we're always looking at what other players are doing and seeing if we can learn from them. Maybe someone hits his driver better than you, or putts better than you. I'll always see if they're doing something I'm not. Mentally it's the same story. I learned from watching José María Olázabal win the Masters. He didn't hit one shot on the last couple of days that he wasn't 100 per cent mentally ready for. You could see him standing behind the ball and his eyes were going from the ball to the target and back again. He could see the trajectory of the shot in his mind. If it wasn't what he wanted to see, he wouldn't hit the shot. That happened on the 16th on Sunday. He was starting to address the ball and suddenly he stepped away. You could tell he was thinking, 'No, I'm not ready.' Then he went through his routine again and you could almost see it in his face: 'Right, now I've got it.' And he hit a fantastic shot.

JESPER ON ...
JUDGING WIND DIRECTION

When I'm hitting balls on the range before a round I get a copy of the course map and draw an arrow indicating the wind direction. I can then refer to that map on the golf course and always know which way the wind is blowing. On a tree-lined course, where the wind can swirl and some teeing areas are sheltered, that can be a real help.

Loosening up before a round with a heavily-weighted club is standard procedure for Jesper. It helps him stretch his golfing muscles.

ON THE TEE, JESPER LOOSENS UP WITH AN UNFEASIBLY HEAVY GOLF CLUB WEIGHTED WITH LEAD, WHICH SEEMS LIKE A GOOD IDEA

He crunches the ball and it fizzes off on a low trajectory, coming to rest 274 yards away. His reaction, a slight moan of dissatisfaction, I take to be a very ominous sign.

There is an immediate upturn in my fortunes. Not because we've located my ball, which is in a deservingly desperate spot and needs to be retrieved by hand from behind a wire fence, but because Jesper allows me the most generous free drop ever witnessed in the Royal & Ancient game, an underarm lob into a relatively inviting patch of semi-rough. Call it a mulligan. A tentatively struck 8-iron finds the fringe of the green and I chip and putt for what you might loosely describe as a par, which is good enough for a half. I sheepishly walk to the next tee.

On the third hole, a woeful sand-wedge from 70 yards (a speciality of mine, I like to think) is the unlikely trigger for the first compliment of the day. With my ball having crept to within eight yards of the green, I reach for my putter and manage to cosy the ball up virtually stone dead. Jesper says, 'That's a typical example of where amateurs go wrong.' I'm shocked, since I thought it wasn't a bad effort. But then he adds, 'Putting from off the green is the right

shot there. I'd have putted it, too.'

The trouble is, he doesn't need to. Having made his first ball change back on the tee (Jesper routinely takes a new ball every three holes) he has creamed his drive and a crisp approach to eight feet yields a comfortable birdie. He also birdies the next hole, hitting a stunning 4-iron from 190 yards.

I think it is here during his ball's journey from the clubface to the green that it really dawns on me just how wide the gulf in ability is. Our club selections will turn out to be fairly similar all the way round (although saying that, Jesper revealed that his irons are set up one-and-a-half clubs weaker, because his ball-flight had become too piercing) but the difference in strike is obvious. His iron shots are struck so solidly, producing a fizzing and soaring trajectory that you just don't see at club level. To use the old cliché, so many of his approach shots 'never leave the flag'.

It's not just that, though. It's the sheer variety in his iron play. 'I like to look at a shot then try to get a feeling for it in my practice swing,' Jesper explains. 'I might be playing a draw for 12 holes then I'll stand over a shot and think, "Oh, this looks perfect for a

The long grass is perhaps the only occasion in our round where I feel more comfortable than Jesper – I'm more used to this predicament than he is.

fade", and I'll go with that. Or I might see a knock-down shot and hit that.' He calls it 'a library of swing feelings'. I frequently notice that he makes practice swings while keeping his eyes all the time focused on the target, not the ground. I can almost see him mentally sifting through his library until a suitable shot comes to mind. Then he is ready to hit.

Meanwhile, things are looking decidedly grim in the Newell camp. Two down after six. The halfway hut beckons, though, and I console myself with the thought of what a bacon sarnie and a bottle of Coke might do for my game. Jesper has cheese and tomato on white, with a can of ginger beer.

The next hole is a tough par 3, 228 yards to the pin and plenty of trouble either side. Jesper nails a 3-iron that couldn't have looked more perfect. Only an unlucky first bounce can deflect it from its

JESPER ON ...
COURSE MANAGEMENT

I'm much better than I used to be. I used to be terrible. A few years back if I thought I had even a slight chance of making it in two on a long par 5 I'd go for it, whatever the risk. Now I'll think about it first.

JESPER ON ...
PUTTING FROM OFF THE GREEN

Putting from just off the green is the right shot. It's easy to knock it stone dead with a putter, but you'd have to do well to chip it that close.

Rangefinder binoculars help Jesper work out yardages during his practice rounds. They're not allowed in actual competition.

JESPER ON ...
DRIVING THE BALL

I don't think of my driving as a real strength in my game. The US Open isn't really my favourite cup of tea, since the focus is so much on hitting it straight. I sometimes think they may as well have red stakes lining the fairways because if you go into the rough it's almost certainly a dropped shot. Most of the time I drive at about 75 per cent of full power. If the course is long and the rough isn't too bad I might go a little harder. But there's no need most of the time. The shape is more important than the distance. Saying that, there are some occasions where I feel best off just giving it a rip. Like when I won the Greensboro Open in 1999. I was a bit wild off the tee that day, so I figured if I was going to miss the fairway I might as well be as far up in the rough as possible. I could make the green from there.

inevitable path towards the flag. I sense he may be starting to feel sorry for me because, caught between clubs, I ask to borrow his 5-wood (another rule goes out of the window) and he agrees. We halve it in three.

Receiving a stroke on the penultimate hole, I manage to sneak a win to take the match down the last, which turns out to be a comedy of errors. I manage to find another snap-hook from my own personal library of swing feelings. Jesper kindly tacks a path up the left rough, and even duffs a chip to make me feel better. Amid some confusion I halve the match and Jesper suggests a sudden-death play-off on the par-3 10th.

On the tee I shamelessly listen in on him and his caddie trying to deduce the yardage with his rangefinder binoculars, a gadget he carries with him

JESPER ON ...
POSITIVE SELF-TALK

It's important on the way round to take a little time to talk to yourself in a positive way. When I'm playing well, it's easy. Even if I miss a green I just think, 'Oh well, I'll just have to get it up and down.' It's simple, no problem. When I'm struggling, it's different. It's easy to think, 'Damn, another bogey coming up.' That's what you have to watch out for. The mind is strong and if you think about something then it usually happens. You have to be very positive with your self-talk. If things are going really bad it often pays to just snap out of it and send your mind somewhere else. Think of something completely different — look at the scenery, have a joke, even think about what you're having for dinner.

I THINK IT IS HERE DURING HIS BALL'S JOURNEY FROM THE CLUBFACE TO THE GREEN THAT IT REALLY DAWNS ON ME JUST HOW WIDE THE GULF IN ABILITY IS

on practice rounds and even on the practice ground to determine the exact distance of the flags and marker boards. It's exactly 131 yards to the flag, a definite wedge for Jesper who knows exactly how far he hits every club. He knocks it to eight feet and

my ball finishes just outside him. With a perfect read from Jesper's caddie, I slot my putt. Could this exert some pressure on the better half in our group? A wry smile in my direction suggests not. Mind you, he's trying hard. Jesper goes through his usual routine, making three or four practice strokes while looking at the hole. He's visualizing the path of the ball to the hole, something he does without fail on every shot. His putt goes in. I knew it would.

As we shake hands, I feel quite content with how the game has gone. Yes, the gulf in ability is pretty

HE'S VISUALIZING THE PATH OF THE BALL TO THE HOLE, SOMETHING HE DOES WITHOUT FAIL ON EVERY SHOT. HIS PUTT GOES IN

vast. His iron play was indeed on another planet. And even though a couple of my drives went past his, the more telling fact is that his worst drive was scarcely any different from his best, whereas mine were a mixed bag of good, average and plain awful. But I hadn't made a fool of myself and I'd given him a half-decent game.

In the car on the way home, though, reflecting on the game, I had to accept that I'd actually lost fair and square. Without that rogue drop at the 1st we would have shaken hands a couple of holes earlier. But who am I to shun the generosity of an all-round nice man who took pity on me after my shaky opening gambit? Jesper, I'll take the half, thank you very much, and say thanks for the game. It was, as they say, a real education.

JESPER ON ...
PLAYING THE CHIP-AND-RUN OUT OF ROUGH

Better to play these chip-and-run shots out of rough with a lofted club and hood the clubface, as the toe will push some of the grass out of the way as it approaches impact and you can get a better strike. Plus it's a more positive shot in the way you hit it. If you go with an 8-iron you tend to be more tentative and the face can more easily get snagged in the grass. First identify your landing target and then focus on that spot. Once you've visualized that you can ignore the target and just land the ball on your spot. That half of the shot you have control over. Let the other half take care of itself.

Playing with a golfer of Jesper's calibre is a real education in every department of the game, mental and physical.

LAURA DAVIES

When you're trying to get a golfing superstar out of bed at the ungodly hour of 5 a.m. on one of their few precious days off, you had better have a good excuse. For Laura Davies, it was the enticement of flying to Scotland for the day and playing the startling Loch Lomond course. The fact that she had to take me with her could have written the whole deal off, but the pull of tackling one of the finest courses in the country (and one she had not seen before) was too great.

LAURA ON ... HOW TO PICK A LINE FOR YOUR DRIVE

I never pick a point the same distance I'm trying to hit it, I always pick a point in the distance, and usually two points to aim between, like two trees at fairway distance apart. Then I focus on them, and then probably go and block it into the bunker anyway!

ANYONE WHO HAS WATCHED LAURA CLOSE UP CAN'T FAIL TO BE IMPRESSED BY HER UNORTHODOX BUT TOTALLY NATURAL SWING, WHICH DOESN'T SPARE THE HORSEPOWER

Her globetrotting lifestyle has obviously prepared her for the ordeal since she looks fresh and fit for action as we cruise in through the stone gates of this magnificent estate in one of the club's gleaming Range Rovers. My golfing tastebuds tingle as soon as I see the unbelievably green swathes of fairway meandering through the trees, and Laura, in her typically understated way, grins and echoes my thoughts. 'Doesn't look too shabby,' she says.

After meeting seemingly the entire staff, all with smiles as wide as the shimmering loch, being taken aback by the locker rooms I would happily have slept in, and a reviving cup of coffee, we crunch our way along the winding gravel path to the 1st tee. The offer of a warm-up on the range was declined by Laura who cheerily admitted she rarely practises: 'What's a warm-up? I never have

a practice round either, unless it's the US Open.' Her comments were a little to my chagrin, as I usually creak like a pirate ship if I haven't had at least a couple of wild swipes before setting off.

In all other respects the scene couldn't be more perfect for me. I harangue her into giving me shots, putting a few feeble excuses her way regarding my recent form, and magnanimously she decides on six. She has also settled for a mixture of the championship and medal tees at a shade over 6,700 yards, 600 or so more than she usually plays on tour, and to add to that yardage the ground is as soggy as a dunked biscuit.

Strangely I don't feel nervous – apprehensive about my play, yes, but not nervous, considering I'm teeing it up with one of the legends of the game. Laura is friendly and quiet, not at all an 'I'm a star' kind of woman. I was at ease

Although her power play is
the most obvious strength
in Laura's golf, she has an
excellent short game to
back it up.

LAURA ON ... THE SHORT GAME

When it's on, mine is one of the better short games, but a lot depends on how you
are putting. It's much easier for your short game to be on song if you are confident
of holing your putts. If you are struggling on the greens, then it puts pressure on
even the best short game. It might come as a shock to some but I spend most of
my practice time hitting chips and putts. A good short game can save you.

Although her power play is
the most obvious strength
in Laura's golf, she has an
excellent short game to
back it up.

I ASKED HER CADDIE TO KEEP A NOTE OF HER YARDAGES TO THE GREENS AND THE CLUBS SHE HIT. IT MAKES SOBER READING FOR THOSE WHO THINK WOMEN'S GOLF IS PAT-PAT

LAURA ON ... WHAT TO LOOK FOR ON A COURSE YOU DON'T KNOW

Hopefully most people should have an idea of how far they hit the ball. They should use that to plan their shots. Without the luxury of a caddie, you should use a yardage chart to find out distances to fairway bunkers and carries over trouble. You should know your limitations, and most of the time play the safer shot of the few options you have.

immediately, if not quite at peace with myself yet. Laura is as relaxed and cool as a Des Lynam interview, making no amateur excuses such as 'Ooh, I'm stiff today', 'Haven't played for a month' or 'I must get a new driver, I haven't hit this one properly for years.'

On a grey, mizzly morning turning into a flashing sun-and-cloud day, she strikes a stupendous low cut under and around a tree from 197 yards out to 8 feet on the 1st. Unfortunately, her Achilles heel of late, putting, surfaces again and she misses the birdie.

Anyone who has watched Laura close up can't fail to be impressed by her unorthodox but totally natural swing, which in raw, athletic terms doesn't spare the horsepower. She has a refreshing attitude to golf – it only becomes a chore if she's not putting the way she knows she can – and fun is at the heart of what she does. Some might say she's careless, but if you look more deeply at it,

Laura's game is a mixture of flair, power and natural ability, which enables her to play shots like this long-iron cut around a tree.

her game is a head-on collision with the course – swashbuckling and cavalier.

As we rattle along – there's no messing about with Laura; slow play gets to her at times – we chat and joke, and generally life looks rosy. Despite Laura not firing on all cylinders, her putts continually tiptoeing around the hole, you can still see the talent flooding from her. I know she's long – not only is it well documented, I've seen it first-hand before – but never have I had the chance to make direct comparisons. It is quite startling to witness. She has a strange approach. No practice swings, she just stands a long way from the ball with the clubhead at least six inches inside it. Gradually she edges in, until after a final reach and a shuffling of the feet towards the ball, she fires. Whooosh!

I asked her caddie John to keep a note of her yardages to the greens and the clubs she hit. It makes sober reading for all those who think women's golf is pat-pat. Laura struck a 3-iron from 217 yards out at the 3rd, an 8-iron at the

'WHAT'S A WARM-UP? I NEVER HAVE A PRACTICE ROUND EITHER, UNLESS IT'S THE US OPEN.'

155-yard 8th, and she went for the 330-yard par-4 14th over the marsh. It is awesome to watch, and there is a joyful abandon about her game.

Unfortunately nothing will drop for her. She knows it's just a matter of time before the putts start falling again. It has been a continual problem over the last couple of seasons. Putts that are seemingly destined for the bottom of the cup tire at the last second, run purposefully through the break or just go tantalizingly close. 'I'm not worried,' she reassures me, 'just a bit frustrated. I know it will turn around – you can see how close it is.' I can.

If putting is the weakness (she knows where she stands in the putting stats) her long irons are her strength. They have a searing quality, and when asked why they are so strong, Laura ventures,

'It's because I hit them everywhere. I can't use my driver because the courses are so short. The first thing I look for on a course is the length, because if it's 6,400 yards then I think, "Yeah, I like this place already."'

It's because of this prodigious hitting (along with the 54 tournament wins worldwide) that she is revered and admired, yet while she has an undeniable presence rather like a Seve or a Norman, she is still happy-go-lucky and humble. It is interesting to see how everyone scurrying around the back of the 9th tee outside the clubhouse stops to watch Laura tee off. They keep their distance but you can tell there's intrigue and an amused respect in their faces as she crashes a 3-iron away. She is held in very high regard in golfing circles. My chest metaphorically puffs out at the thought that I'm strutting the fairways with the world's most famous lady golfer, but never does she make me feel small or insignificant.

Her influence has a magical effect on my game. I play out of my skin; I'm almost apologetic about

LAURA ON ...

NERVES
The most nervous I've been is when I was drawn to play with Arnold Palmer at Fred Couples' event. I could hardly take the club back, and I knobbled a few drives. He was brilliant, though, and kept on telling me not to worry and just play. He is a legend. I now understand why my pro-am partners get so nervous.

THINKING POSITIVELY
Most amateurs stand on the tee, look down the hole and think to themselves, 'I don't want to go there or there.' But professionals look and say, 'Where do I want to go?' That is half the battle. If more amateurs could focus on where they wanted to hit it rather than where they didn't, they would get better results. Personally, I sometimes force myself to focus by playing a driver off the deck. I know that if I don't concentrate and hit it perfectly I could make a fool of myself.

HOW TO COPE WITH PRESSURE DOWN THE STRETCH
I just play and hope it works out. I don't think there is anything you can do to combat nerves. Even though you might feel bad, just get on with it. Don't forget, everyone gets nervous. The champions are those who can cope best. I'm always thinking positive about the last hole — I'm looking for a birdie, it's not just about finishing my round.

LAURA ON ... WHAT YOU CAN LEARN FROM HER GAME

Anything you want to. There is no one thing. I learn from other pros all the time. I love to watch Seve's short game, and Langer's long irons. I like to look at the lack of fear when he is faced with a 1-iron into a guarded pin – he doesn't worry, he just hits it. I learn from someone every day. I would advise any amateur to watch players, pick out their best points and try to lock them away in your mind.

Laura takes this unexpected defeat with good grace.

Laura unleashes another fearsome long-iron shot, although her round today is marred by a disappointing putting performance.

my new-found form. This is not how the script was meant to go. Her extraordinary game is there to be seen, but it's just one of those days where the putts don't drop. On the 13th green, with the six shots she gave me taking their toll, she shakes my hand and accepts defeat in typically good humour. I can tell she's a little annoyed, but she never makes me feel like a pariah. Instead, she compliments me on my play. Laura even has the heart for a quip: 'Even when you knocked it into Sherwood Forest you came out with a birdie. Amazing.'

'Just call me Robin Hood,' I reply.

'Yeah, stealing from the rich!'

Happily, we don't walk in when the game is over, instead completing the full 18 holes, which gives me the opportunity to marvel further at her golf. She rifles a glorious 1-iron past me at the 15th, hits a towering draw into a tight flag at the wondrous 17th and unleashes her trademark driver 265 yards into the wind at the home hole which glides down the lochside towards the impeccable clubhouse. It's great stuff.

MARK JAMES

It is a bitterly cold morning in Yorkshire. The scene is Ilkley Golf Club car park, elevated high above the 1st fairway. There is frost on the ground and fog in the air. It seems an unlikely place for a match against the 1999 European Ryder Cup captain, Mark James, an 18-time winner on tour and accumulator of more than £3 million in prize money. But actually this is very much home turf for Mark. He lives just a short drive down the road and is an honorary member of the club.

A frosty foggy morning on a deserted golf course in the hills of Yorkshire is the setting for this match against Europe's former Ryder Cup captain Mark James.

As we change our shoes up against the boot of Mark's smart BMW, handicaps are discussed. I play the sympathy card, revealing that in my game against Ernie Els I received 'only' four shots. Mark agrees this is not very generous (good) and says he will play off +2 and give me five shots (not so good). As he hands me a scorecard and my visitor's green fee sticker, I note that two of those five shots will come in the first four holes – perhaps an opportunity to get my cold, runny nose in front for a precious early advantage.

In the circumstances it all looks quite encouraging. Mark claims to play only ten non-competitive rounds a year, and I doubt too many of those take place on crispy-frosty turf. I, on the other hand, have played more games than I can remember in such conditions, enduring the futility of winter foursomes where the ball bounces with all the predictability of Camelot's lottery balls pinging around in their glass box. This is also Mark's first game of golf in three months, which I take to be a good sign. I sense the faint whiff of hope in the air.

A fine striker of the ball with every club in the bag, Mark clips the ball off the crispy turf with characteristic precision.

On the 1st tee Mark groans with the effort of his first practice swing on a freezing-cold morning, but then spanks a driver down the middle with a hint of draw. It is an ominously good start, and it sets the pattern for the early stages of our encounter. Mark hits the first four greens in regulation and pars each hole – quite an achievement given that the ground is hard and bobbly in the shade, softening in the sunny patches, and the greens are what Mark describes as '2.3 on the stimpmeter'. I have not adapted to the conditions quite so readily and I find myself three down after four holes. There goes my early-advantage game plan!

Mark is quick to get to the 5th tee and carefully studies his yardage chart. Although he has no caddie, preferring today to carry his own bag, he confesses that he can't club by sight any more. On each tee he paces out the distance from the back markers to the winter tees, and constantly refers to his yardage chart on the fairway. It is intriguing to watch, because Mark is known as a great course manager. He tells me it's his biggest strength. 'People go on about some of the really top players being great course managers, but it's easy when you're hitting the ball straight all the time. My golden rule is that if I'm not certain I can pull off a shot, it's better not to go for it. On par 5s you see a lot of pros make mistakes through trying to force a birdie. When you're playing poorly these holes are more dangerous, because there's more yards in which to get into trouble.'

Luckily for me, today Mark is happy to share his insights with his opponent and I use them to good effect, halving the next two holes and steadying a previously very rocky ship. The 7th hole, the Beacon, shines an apt ray of hope on my fortunes. The ground has softened under the pale winter sunshine and Mark's birdie putt takes the worst bobble I have ever seen on a golf course, hopping at least three inches into the air and grinding to a halt six feet short of the hole. His par putt is then similarly afflicted. That double-bobble bogey puts me back to just two down and it stays that way until the turn.

At least, I think to myself, utter humiliation has been averted. To add to that I am thoroughly enjoying watching the way Mark plays the game, even though he's not in prime form. His technique may look slightly unconventional, but there is nothing mechanical about it. From close range it comes across as not only effective but also very

Mark confesses he's never really suffered from nerves and says it's easier to stay calm if you keep a sense of perspective.

MARK ON ...
THE BEST TIP I EVER HEARD

The best tip I've ever come across is to line the clubface up to the target before you take your stance with your feet. That's very important, because a slight change in the address position is often what causes golfers to play badly. Overall, I think you can get too complicated with teaching, because methods are often misinterpreted. The best tips tend to be simple and can be applied to a lot of people. I think John Jacobs is good, he's very straightforward. David Leadbetter is also a very good teacher. But I think when he had his disciples out teaching his method it didn't work so well. I think you need to have your own eye on something and teach people yourself. You're either good at it or you're not.

MARK ON ... CONSISTENT PITCHING

If I ever start hitting pitch shots badly I immediately know I'm easing up on the downswing and scooping under the ball a bit. This is where a lot of amateurs go wrong, too. I always work on accelerating through and not flipping with the right hand, making sure I maintain the late hit even on a short shot. That's a good swing thought. I think it's also best to play as many pitch shots as possible with the same club, so you develop some confidence. Unless there's a lot of wind, I always use a lob-wedge.

repeatable – the legacy of remaining true to one coach, Gavin Christie, since he was 12 years old. 'Gavin basically gave me my swing,' Mark says. 'Well, the good bits, anyway!' Mark thus knows his swing inside out and relies on trust and feel, two powerful allies. To me his driving seems dependable – not overly long, but very controlled – and his iron play is among his biggest strengths. Not only does he like to shape the ball both ways,

but also high and low as required.

Both of us find the green on the 10th and we walk up to find that the hole is cut exactly one yard on from the front, presumably to protect the putting surface in such unfavourable ground conditions. This pin position amuses Mark, as professional caddies always give their player the exact yardage in two parts: the distance to the front of the green and then a number from the

HIS TECHNIQUE MAY LOOK SLIGHTLY UNCONVENTIONAL, BUT THERE IS NOTHING MECHANICAL ABOUT IT. FROM CLOSE RANGE IT COMES ACROSS AS EFFECTIVE AND VERY REPEATABLE

front to the flag. 'One-fifty to the front,' he quips, 'one yard on!' We have a laugh about how certain players on tour might react to such a pin placement, but three putts later my smile is gone. As we walk off the green I complain to Mark that there is surely nothing more depressing in golf than a miserable three-putt, and he sympathizes. 'Slow play can be pretty irritating,' he adds, 'but it's not in the same galaxy as putting badly.'

There's no danger of Mark becoming even mildly rattled by his putting today though; not even the best stroke in the world could produce a smooth roll on these surfaces. If anything, he finds it amusing. As we chat on the way round I discover that not much seems to bother him, not even nerves. 'To be honest, I've never really been too stricken with nerves. Obviously you have to concentrate, but I think mentally you have to take the pressure off yourself and keep a sense of proportion. Don't panic, take your time and play your normal game. People make it more complicated than it is. Some sports psychologists certainly help to make it more complicated than it is.' He does concede that playing the Ryder Cup is a test. 'You see what you're made of in the Ryder

MARK ON ... SLOWING DOWN YOUR SWING

In pro ams I tend to see all kinds of faults, but often the root cause is the same. Loss of rhythm. When golfers with strange swings, maybe a loop of some kind at the top of the backswing, start playing badly it's nearly always because they get a little quick and don't give themselves time for their loop to come out. So I often get them to slow down, especially from the top of the backswing into their downswing.

Mark can shape the ball either way through the air, but his preferred shot is the draw.

weekend, shot two great rounds and won the tournament. Nick Faldo used to be the same. People would talk about his long game, but his short game was just phenomenal. He could shoot a decent score playing badly.'

On the next, Mark's only loose drive of the day enables me to capitalize on my final shot-hole, but time is running out and I can reduce the deficit no further. The end comes on the next green, and back in the car park I tot up the scores. Mark has got round in 71; only the uneven greens prevented him from being at least a couple under par. Throughout the round he has been a gentleman, showing genuine interest in both me and my golf. It's a quality many amateur golfers have experienced in Mark's company over the years. 'I never mind playing in pro ams,' he reveals. 'The only problem is that people sometimes expect too much. They want you to turn their 20-handicap into a 3-handicap in the space of 18 holes. But as long as people pick up when they're out of a hole and they're good company, I don't have a problem.'

Mark's appetite for the game is undiminished after 25 years on tour and he is physically fitter now than ever, despite treatment for cancer at the end of 2000 which mercifully was successful and means he is out again doing what he's best at –

Keeping a smooth rhythm to the swing is one of Mark's keys to consistent golf, a tip he often gives to amateurs.

Cup. But I don't think it makes you a better player, certainly not in my case. I was crap before and I was crap afterwards!' But when he won his first tournament in Zambia in 1977 he played the back nine in six under par to win by two. Clearly, people have their own interpretations of crap.

By the 11th Mark has yet to miss a fairway, and although he is less than pleased with this particular effort, the ball flies pretty much dead straight down the middle, maybe 20 yards shorter than a solid hit.

'It's great when your bad shots are that respectable,' I say to him.

He agrees, and reveals that he believes this is one of Lee Westwood's great strengths. 'I played with him in the first two rounds of a tournament last year and he wasn't playing that great, but he didn't hit a single really destructive shot and went 72, 68. Then he started playing better at the

HE DOES CONCEDE THAT PLAYING THE RYDER CUP IS A TEST. 'YOU SEE WHAT YOU'RE MADE OF IN THE RYDER CUP. BUT I DON'T THINK IT MAKES YOU A BETTER PLAYER'

MARK ON... SHAPING YOUR IRON SHOTS

Iron play is one of my strengths. I can shape the ball fairly well and move it both ways, which I think is an advantage. If I have the choice I draw it, and I always practise a draw because I think people who can draw it can usually also fade it, whereas people who fade it generally have trouble with the draw. During a round I try to make myself do both, because I find that if I go even ten holes without hitting a fade I won't want to do it when one is required. However, I think handicap golfers need to develop a consistent shape of shot before they start getting fancy. Once that's done, make sure you shape shots by changing your set-up, not your swing. For a fade, I just aim left and open the clubface a bit. I might also put the ball a little forward in my stance, making it easier to come across it through impact. With a draw the clubface will be square or even a fraction closed. That method should work for everyone.

playing professional golf. 'The biggest problem with being a tour pro,' he confesses, 'is the travelling. But I'm quite good at it. I go into what my wife calls my "travel coma". I'm also lucky that I'm not a nervous flier, like a lot of golfers are.' Mark certainly has no plans for retirement and intends to keep on playing into the senior tours. 'There's too much money to be made,' he says. 'This is my job and I'm out there to make as much as I can.'

Unfortunately, this game cannot be described as one of Mark's more profitable outings. Indeed, he makes a comfortable loss. He picks up the tab for my green fee and then whisks the photographer and me off for lunch at a Little Chef down the road. Got his feet on the ground, has Mark.

MARK ON... SMARTER PRACTISING

If you don't feel like hitting balls on a particular day, don't bother. It probably won't do you any good. But when you do practise, start with wedge shots and work your way through to the mid-irons. If you jump into the gorilla stuff too quickly you won't have any rhythm. Build rhythm slowly and work up to the long clubs over the space of 40 or 50 balls, not 11 or 12. I mean, we're all the same – even on tour we like to give it a slash with the driver. But it's best if you give it a slash with good rhythm!

On home turf, there was only ever going to be one winner, and Mark's round of 71 was a fine score in view of the wintry conditions.

MICHAEL CAMPBELL

There are a lot of professional golfers who play nicely, but don't blow your socks off with their ball-striking. Not Michael Campbell. This powerfully built Kiwi is impressive to watch, actually more impressive than his record suggests.

He has a rock-solid base as he stands to the ball. He is solidly built, too, part of which is natural and part of which is the result of a punishing exercise regime, which seems an integral part of all top professional sport these days. 'Every day I do a lot of stretching, lots of work on my abdominals,' Michael says, entering territory I am not familiar with. 'I also do a lot of cardio exercise,' he adds. 'I always work out after I've played, and sometimes before my round as well. I think it helps me play better. I try to get my heart rate up to 150 beats per minute for 30 minutes or so, that gets the endorphins going through my body. When I get to the golf course I feel great, really energized and ready to go.'

There certainly is a lot of energy generated in Michael's swing, and the golf ball bears the full brunt of it. He hasn't played for three weeks, literally not touched a club, but typically and worryingly for me his game shows no signs of a lay-off. After a steady opening par 4, Michael's birdie on the 2nd is ominously good – a nailed drive, a fizzing 4-iron and an easy two-putt. It sure does look good.

On the 3rd he pulls his driver out of the bag without even looking down the fairway to assess the hole and, after the customary couple of vigorous waggles, torpedoes his Nike ball into the grey Sussex sky. A punchy 7-iron straight over the flag leaves him with a none-too-appealing 30-footer downhill, but he slots that for another birdie. 'The statistics say my putting is my main

Michael torpedoes another drive into the grey Sussex sky, displaying power that makes him impressive to watch.

'I ALSO DO A LOT OF CARDIO EXERCISE,' HE ADDS. 'I ALWAYS WORK OUT AFTER I'VE PLAYED, AND SOMETIMES BEFORE MY ROUND AS WELL. I THINK IT HELPS ME PLAY BETTER.'

strength, and I'd go along with that,' he observes. 'More than anything else it's my putting that's helped me do well over the last few years.'

He then hits a ridiculously impressive 2-iron into the teeth of a very un-springlike stiff breeze. The ball thuds down on the green 210 yards away. Now I'm rattled. Intimidation is a word bandied about a lot on the US and European tours, but I don't think professionals know the meaning of the word. They should try being this far out of their depth, like I am now, then maybe they'd understand what intimidation really feels like. Today I'm going down, big time!

The evidence is overwhelming. Every swing from 100 yards upwards seems to produce a heavy hit, courtesy of the simplest of actions.

Michael is a powerfully built athlete and gives every shot outside the 100-yard range a serious thump.

Michael's arms and body seem perfectly connected as he turns back and through. To be honest, I've seldom seen the process of hitting a ball well appear so natural, and that pretty much reflects his view of the game. Michael's not a technically minded player, even though he knows what feels right and what doesn't. 'I try to write things down and make mental notes, whether it's positive or negative,' he explains. 'It's usually nothing too in-depth, but it might be a certain feeling I had on a particular day that helped me play well. Or it might be something I noticed I felt when I was playing badly. Either way these little swing thoughts are handy to look back on.'

If I were hazarding a guess, today is a 'good swing thought day' for Michael. Everything is coming out of the middle of the bat and he seems to be almost swept along by the momentum of one good shot after another. This is the sort of form that makes him a formidable force on his day.

Although he can blow a little cold some weeks,

MICHAEL ON ... HIS SWING

Old habits always have a tendency to creep back into your golf swing. It's the same with every professional. The most common thing I do wrong is I tend to take the club back on the outside in my backswing, then let the club get way too flat at the top. Every time I hit a bad shot it's because of that one bad habit. I've had that trouble ever since I was a kid. So I'm constantly working on getting the club going back in more of a straight line, then I can hinge my wrists so the club is more upright and in better balance

halfway back. That's kind of what I'm trying to rehearse in my pre-swing waggle of the clubhead at address. It's pretty simple really. But I've always liked to work on simple things in my swing. That's how I play my best golf. To stop any bad habits creeping back into my game, I decided I would see my coach Jonathan Yarwood every three to four weeks. That way we can keep an eye on things and make sure everything is in the right place in my swing.

he's at the level we all anticipated he would be when he almost won the Open at St Andrews in 1995. He's challenging for top honours in Europe and climbed to number 15 in the world, just half a point outside the elite top 10 in 2001. It's all the more creditable as he's had to haul himself back from a bleak couple of years. But he's not yet satisfied. Michael is determined to keep climbing, and he knows the best way to achieve that. 'I see myself playing pretty much full time in the States,' he reveals. 'It's easier for me to pick up my hat and base myself somewhere else because I'm from Down Under. For someone like Colin

JONATHAN YARWOOD ON ... MICHAEL'S SWING

Michael got injured at the beginning of 1996 and was struggling to recapture his swing and his form, so he started experimenting and asking too many people for their opinions. While there's merit in what most teachers say, all those different ideas don't necessarily fit together and you can easily get into a lot of trouble. The further down that track you go, the worse it gets, because you're searching for more and more information. Before you know it you've lost everything that made your swing good in the first place. That's basically what happened to Michael, which is why he started playing poorly. It got so bad that at the end of 1997 he had no tour card. He'd hit the wall. That's when he came over to Florida and we started working together. Right then we designed a blueprint of what his swing should be like and we've stuck to that goal ever since.

Obviously Michael's got tons of talent. He's got a great physique for golf. He's got a very low centre of gravity, with a stocky physique and short arms. You can develop a very simple swing on foundations like that. That's what we set out to achieve. Michael now has a very simple swing, where the club stays virtually on the same plane back and down. It's also a very repetitive action. If things do get a little out of place we see each other regularly enough to be able to quickly put them back.

I think the average player can learn a lot from a swing like Michael's. The simplicity is the thing. If you take care in your set-up and make sure you're standing properly you have a far better chance of developing a sound golf swing. Michael's proof of that. We spent a lot of time making sure he was standing correctly, aiming correctly, with a good grip and posture. And look how simple the golf swing can actually be — it's just a turn and a hinge to set the club and a turn and a hinge on the way through.

A Ferrari is Michael's preferred set of wheels, but today he has to settle for the more sedate pace of a golf buggy.

Montgomerie, Darren Clarke or Lee Westwood it's harder, because they're obviously from this part of the world. I'll still come over here and play the tournaments I enjoy. There are six or seven events in Europe that are fantastic, as good as anything else in the world. The big tournaments in the States are not necessarily any better than the biggest events in Europe, it's just that there are more of them. Week in week out, the quality

is better.' So that's where the future lies for this Kiwi, but Michael hasn't yet decided when that big move across the pond will take place. He has some unfinished business in Europe. 'I want to fulfil a few goals first, like winning the Order of Merit, for one thing. But I definitely will make the move. I want to throw myself in at the deep end to see how good I can get. Thirty years down the track I don't want to be sitting in my rocking

chair saying, "Oh, I wish I'd gone and tried that." I've got nothing to lose. My kids are still young, so if it doesn't work out after three or four years we'll just come back.'

Time to stop talking and start playing again. The 6th is a refreshingly short par 4. Michael tries to boom one on to the green, but the ball drifts very slightly left and topples off the fairway into some rough. While he's looking for his ball, I

Behind the shades is a cool customer who keeps his emotions in check, on and off the golf course.

hit my second shot to within a foot of the hole. He looks up to see my ball on the green and is clearly suspicious. He shouts across, 'Did you throw that, or what?' No, but it may come to that. Mind you, I may throw in the towel first.

By the turn, I've been in the water for a triple-bogey and I conclude the front nine with the sort of double-bogey six that makes grown men cry. Michael, meanwhile, is cruising. He's hitting the ball so hard with his driver it's frankly quite frightening – and he hasn't even had the good nature to spray one off line yet. He's rifling his iron shots into the middle of the greens and putting beautifully. All in all, I couldn't feel more helpless if Jonah Lomu were running towards me with his pants on fire.

After ten holes, having just notched up birdie number four, Michael feels his lead and his card are sufficiently secure to give me a lesson on chipping. 'People complicate this game too much. With chipping you've got to keep it as simple as possible. Whenever you can, just play the ball off

your back foot with the hands forward and use very little wrist break in your swing.' I try it. It works.

Michael's in the kind of groove where it's actually hard to imagine him hitting anything remotely resembling a stray shot. Even if he does, it's not going to make any difference to the outcome of the match and it certainly won't faze him. Behind those wrap-around shades are the eyes of a poker player. He gives nothing away. Hard to read, to be honest. He's the same in tournaments and, indeed, in life. It's just the way he is. 'I don't tend to show my emotions all that well,' he remarks. 'Just ask my wife! I tend to hide what I'm thinking. I have lost it a few times on the golf course, but not very often. And it takes a lot for me to lose it, and even then it doesn't last long. I know it sounds like a cliché but I really feel I'm lucky to be playing this game. There are a lot of people out there far less fortunate than me. If things aren't going that great some days, big deal! I just think occasionally you have to stop and smell the flowers and keep things in perspective.' Michael seems utterly genuine when he expresses such sentiments, which is pleasing to know because, let's be honest, there are some 24-carat whingebags at the top of every sport. Not Michael, though. I get the feeling that not much worries him. And why should it? When you chat to him, you realize he's got life sussed. 'I'll play the next ten years, work hard, give it 110 per cent and see how far I can get in the game,' he says. 'Then I'm going to retire, take life easy and enjoy myself.'

The more immediate future brings Michael a couple more birdies, stretching his lead, the best of which is registered on the par-5 14th where a majestic 4-wood airmails his ball to pin high and easy two-putt range.

On the 18th Michael chuckles to himself as he hits his worst drive of the day. Worst is a relative term, though. It's still a 270-yard tonk. And it's only ten yards off the fairway, too, which isn't my

> **'I DON'T TEND TO SHOW MY EMOTIONS ALL THAT WELL,' HE REMARKS. 'JUST ASK MY WIFE! I TEND TO HIDE WHAT I'M THINKING. I HAVE LOST IT A FEW TIMES ON THE GOLF COURSE, BUT NOT VERY OFTEN.'**

idea of wild. But the lie is unkind. Michael peers down at his ball and is unperturbed. A fierce dig with a 6-iron creates an explosion of wet grass and mud, and when the view finally clears his ball is sailing towards the flag. It was not an easy shot and Michael made it look easy, as he does the 25-footer for a closing birdie three. Had this been a boxing match, I'd have been back in the changing room with the smelling salts and an ice pack several hours ago. As it is, we've gone the full distance and the judges are laughing hysterically at their score sheets. Michael is round in a mightily impressive 67. That's five under par from the tournament tees on a miserable, damp, squally day on poor greens which were nothing to do with the greenkeeper and everything to do with a dire English spring. And you know something? He didn't even look like he was trying. It was all so ... how can I put this? So utterly depressing!

Actually, it was a joy to watch, and for once being on the end of a heavy defeat didn't seem too bad after all.

MICHAEL ON ... THE BEST OF EVERYTHING

DRIVING
I would say Monty. I remember a time when he was playing well, we were paired together in a tournament at the Forest of Arden and he shot a 63 in really tough conditions. He was so impressive. There were a few holes where for most players it was basically a lay-up with an iron or a 3-wood, but he hit a driver every time and finished perfect.

IRON PLAY
I was going to say Monty again! But probably Tiger. His iron play is pretty special, not just the way he hits it but also the control he has.

CHIPPING
The best chipper I've ever seen is Ollie, no question. He can hit an incredible variety of shots and he's just lethal from everywhere around the greens.

BUNKER PLAY
Ollie again. He's very impressive. The array of shots he can play out of sand is tremendous.

PUTTING
Tiger, definitely. Everyone talks about how long he is and all that carry-on, but just watch how many vital six- and seven-footers he holes for pars and birdies. His putting really is exceptional, and that's often the difference between him and the rest of the field.

MIGUEL ANGEL JIMÉNEZ

Most people who spend their lives in the shadows tend to squint a little when they walk into the spotlight. Not so Miguel Angel Jiménez, a man whose equilibrium remains undisturbed whether he's cruising down Málaga's seafront in his Ferrari 550 Maranello or holing knee-trembling putts during a Ryder Cup. You rarely know with Miguel quite what mood he's in. His disposition is as steady and consistent as his game; he is unhurried, unflustered, unflappable. He has the demeanour of a man who has his life worked out and is able to put his feet up and sit back with an espresso because of it.

A little local knowledge from the home town hero comes in handy when you've strayed from the straight and narrow.

Such traits, though, are hardly a PR man's dream. I mean, what do we know about Miguel that makes him stand out from the crowd? He is Spanish. Since turning pro in 1982, he has won six times on the European Tour. He has an impressive record in team competitions, having played in the World Cup and the Ryder Cup and having won the Dunhill Cup twice. But despite all that, he was, until his performance in the Ryder Cup at Brookline in 1999, a hopelessly unheralded golfer. Few people knew very much about him, other than the fact that he was inclined to have big hair, a big moustache and a swing that had more planes than BA.

Twenty years in the business, Miguel has been a late developer. If there were those who underestimated his talent two years ago, few do so today. The 37-year-old has risen from obscurity to become a professional sportsman respected on a world level. But has that changed him? Not in the least.

He arrives in his other car, a BMW M3, lugs his pro bag out of the boot and heads for the pro shop. This is familiar territory to a man who as a 15-year-old new to the game spent most daylight hours

mingling with the caddie ranks here at the Parador Málaga Del Golf. Like the Pied Piper of Parador, Miguel is followed to the 1st tee by a group of excited youngsters, two of whom, the sons of the club's manager, have been invited to play with us. This would be fine if they weren't much good, but the fact that they drill their tee shots down the centre of the fairway like a couple of young Seves is disconcerting. It's one thing to come to the lions' den, quite another to be mauled to death

by a couple of his cubs.

As if to put all of us in our place, the lion (that's Miguel) accelerates out of the blocks like a ... well, like a Ferrari 550. He makes a regulation birdie at the par-5 1st and moves to two under with another on the par-4 2nd. While my game clearly needs a visit to the garage, his is purring along as if dwelling in red figures were the easiest thing in the world.

'This is a very nice course,' he comments politely. 'You like this course?'

'Yes, it's very nice,' I reply, although it's a little early to tell and it's clear that Miguel is viewing the layout through rose-tinted glasses. It is his home track after all.

'So what's your best score round here?' I add. At

'HE'S A MAN OF THE PEOPLE. HE DRINKS WITH THE LOCALS, EATS WITH THE LOCALS AND THEY ARE ALL FRIENDS TOGETHER. YOU SEE HIM HERE IN THE BARS. HE MIXES WITH THOSE HE HAS GROWN UP WITH.'

One of Miguel's rare loose shots is tidied up with a neat bunker shot to save par.

two down after two it's a careless question, and one that I regret the instant it comes out.

'Sixty-two,' Miguel replies matter-of-factly. It's a score he produced a few years ago when the Turespaña Masters Open de Andalucía came to town and Miguel thrilled the local crowd by capturing the title.

Born and bred in the Churriana region of Málaga, it's understandable that he's a popular fellow around these parts. Not one of the Jiménez clan – he has seven brothers – has moved more than a few miles from the family home. They all play golf to some level and one of them is the pro at neighbouring Torrequebrada. Roger Sutcliffe is an ex-pat who has lived in Málaga now for several years and things are very much as he describes them. 'He's a man of the people. He drinks with the locals, eats with the locals and they are all friends together. You see him here in the bars. He mixes with those he has grown up with.' Juan Carlos García, whose son Javier is able to outhit Miguel on a number of holes, lets me into a secret. 'Nothing would change Miguel, even if he won the British Open,' he says in a whisper.

By the time we reach the 9th tee, the match is already drifting beyond my reach. I'm still two down and facing the prospect of going three down when my 3-iron to the par 3 is caught by the sea breeze and deposited 50 yards to the right of the target. Miguel also misjudges his approach, coming up ten yards short, so when my sand-wedge finishes within a foot, I feel a rush of relief. There is still hope.

Lost in a moment of cocky oblivion, I call over to my opponent, 'Okay Miguel, down in two for a Ryder Cup half!'

The moustache bristles, the eyes narrow. He pops the ball up into the air, it lands on the front edge of the green, curls gently to the right and drops into the hole. The two boys cheer and I now know what David Feherty meant when he described hope as disappearing over the horizon with his arse on fire.

The halfway hut at Parador is an octagonal box from which various delicacies are sold on little plates. Miguel contents himself by ordering an espresso and unwrapping a large, fat Cuban cigar. He's now three up after my attempt at putting a little pressure on him so magnificently backfired.

'The more pressure, the more I like,' he states quite simply, drawing deeply on his cigar and blowing a big puff of smoke in my face. 'When I started to play golf and I was 15, we always

Miguel's swing may be idiosyncratic but at the moment of impact, where it really matters, he is totally orthodox.

played for something. It teaches you to fight. You can't always expect to win, but when you do that is where your confidence comes from. I joined the tour in 1989, then in my fourth year I won a tournament and my belief in myself kept on growing. I think it was harder to get my card than it has been to keep it. You must, though, put in a lot of work. I hit a thousand balls a week. I love to. Most of the players need to do that, they need to practise.'

If Miguel hadn't worked hard on his game, he

MIGUEL ON ...
THE CHIP FROM HARD PAN

On the 16th, one of the boys pushed his second shot onto a bare lie of dry mud to the right of the green. His attempt at a recovery took the form of an ugly thin that flew across the green causing his brother to dip his head below the parapet of the bunker on the other side. There followed a five-minute time-out in which Miguel explained how to tackle one of the most tricky shots in the game. 'I play the ball well back in my stance, keep my head still and use a firm, brisk stroke that collects the ball and throws it up onto the green,' he said. 'It is very important that you do not let the clubhead overtake the hands, and one of the ways to do this is to keep your wrist action to a bare minimum. Most of the time when you thin the ball, it's because there is too much hand action and you are tending to scoop the ball.'

might still be working at the local garage where he spent three months of his youth sweeping the floor and moving the cars around. 'That's where I learned to drive,' he remembers fondly.

Even with a generous allocation of nine strokes, things take a turn for the worse when Miguel wins the 10th to go four up. His smooth, idiosyncratic swing is holding up well under the pressure of playing from as far back on the tees as the course allows.

Intrigued by this man's monotonous consistency, I ask him on the tee of the par-5 12th what he thinks about when he's over the ball.

'I don't think about anything,' he replies. 'I just get on and play the game. For me everything is about rhythm. I think you should hold the club as lightly as you can and then concentrate on keeping everything smooth. Rhythm is the magic word in golf.' Ironic, then, that a man whose nickname is the Mechanic is a spanner short of a toolkit when it comes to the mechanics of the golf swing. 'I swing more rounded for a draw and more upright for a fade,' he adds. 'It's

HIS DISPOSITION IS AS STEADY AND CONSISTENT AS HIS GAME; HE IS UNHURRIED, UNFLUSTERED, UNFLAPPABLE

simple. Look.' He tees up a couple of balls and sweeps them with equal amounts of draw and fade into the centre of the fairway. In each case his swing looks virtually the same.

Putting the rhythm method into practice, I too launch quite an attractive drive which parks itself just behind Miguel's ball on the fairway. However, while my thoughts on the tee were 'accelerate smoothly', the same cannot be said of the approach. A little too much wheel spin sees the ball veer off the track and into a gravel pit, otherwise known as a bunker.

Relief was shortlived and the end is nigh as Miguel homes in on his fourth birdie of the round on the par-5 16th.

I have been outfoxed, outfought and outclassed, none of which comes as any great surprise, but it has all been done with the minimum of fuss. I didn't really know too much about it until I studied the maths on the scorecard.

We shake hands and Miguel heads off to the beach where his family are waiting for him. I walk to the octagonal hut, put my feet up and order an espresso. This is a leaf out of Miguel's book I could get used to.

Holing putts is something Miguel makes a habit of doing, never more so than when he shot 62 on this course to win the Turespana Masters in 1999.

NICK FALDO

Of all the items you may expect to see in a pro shop, a little metal train is not one of them. It sits on an imaginary track which circles a stand for Shadow Ridge-logoed polo shirts. It has a silver engine the size of two sugar cubes and behind it there are four little carriages in tow. The relevance of such a trinket is not obvious until you move closer to see a $75 price tag and the letters F-A-L-D-O engraved on the side of each piece. Britain's best ever golfer has made a sizeable impact in this Californian neighbourhood, so much so that it seems anything with his name on it might seduce a prospective purchaser.

Nick is a far more relaxed character these days which means the public will get to see a side of his character previously kept under competitive wraps.

HIS NEW COURSE, HIS FIRST IN AMERICA, HAS OPENED TO RAVE REVIEWS, AND THE BUZZ OF EXCITEMENT IS BECOMING MORE PRONOUNCED AS HIS ARRIVAL BECOMES IMMINENT

Nick Faldo is the talk of the town in Palm Desert, which is saying something when you consider that as a golf course designer he is up against such luminaries as Arnold Palmer and Jack Nicklaus. His new course, his first in America, has opened to rave reviews, and the buzz of excitement in the pro shop is becoming more pronounced as his arrival becomes more imminent.

This whistle-stop visit aims to achieve three things: introduce Shadow Ridge to the American press, make some final adjustments to the course and play golf with a journalist from the UK, namely me. The first of those objectives is achieved in a tent on the practice ground, the other two are completed in unison, allowing me a unique insight into the way a designer analyses the strategic subtleties of a golf course.

A sea change has occurred in Nick Faldo. He has got married for a third time, he has moved into a house in Windsor and the chapters of his future biography, the ones that include heroic tales of triumphs in golf's major championships,

have all been written. 'I have rising damp, woodworm and a leaky roof, but lots of character,' he says, referring to his new abode, although you may not have known it. What is noticeable about his attitude is that it has become more relaxed and more open to those around him. He is a friendlier Faldo, a more honest and attentive one. He has also become reflective where once he was resolute.

We tee off. Nick, after a 20-hour flight and a couple of hours in a car, nails it down the middle. I, after a relaxed breakfast and a bucket of balls on the practice ground, knobble a heely one that nips off to investigate the thicker grass to the right.

'I've been on the road 27 years and I've been shocked at how little time I actually get to myself,' he muses as we walk down the fairway. 'Out of 52 weeks it doesn't feel good when I have only 6 spare. I keep thinking that you've got to enjoy it as well. I want to start seeing friends. Sometimes it's embarrassing because they ring you up to suggest getting together and you have to say, "Yes, I'd love to, call me in November." They think it's wicked to arrange dinner in five months' time.' Friendship is something Nick values far more now than he ever did in the past. As a pro golfer in an obsessional quest for major

Inspired by the great Alister Mackenzie, there is no symmetry to them; they twist and turn with the land, forming deep pits that are placed maddeningly close to the golfer's ideal line. So vertical and clean are the edges to these hazards that they create shadows even when the sun is reaching the pinnacle of its route across the sky – hence the name Shadow Ridge.

His mind on the fine detail of the humps and hollows ahead, Nick's game looks as solid as it ever was. He probably doesn't know it, but he has parred the first handful of holes. It's time, perhaps, to draw him out of his designer cocoon.

'It all looks so easy now, but when I watch you in tournaments it seems sometimes that you're trying too hard,' I suggest.

'Well, it will look like that. When you're playing well everything flows – a bit of ballet, ain't it, mate? Then, when it's not going so well you try your ballet and you fall over. When you've got to think about it, it's not as natural, you haven't quite got that same inner confidence to pull off the shots. I loved the way I played at Muirfield in the 1992 Open Championship. "Go

The frustration for Nick nowadays is the lack of ball control compared to his prime, even though he can still hit shots as pretty as this par-3 (left).

Nick surveys his creation and even at this advanced stage, with the golf course finished, continues to suggest minor tweaks to the layout (right).

When he was winning Major championships, few golfers holed out better than Nick. But now his putting is a source of frustration (bottom right).

championships, making friends came well down the priority list. 'When I was coming up it was all one thing, just golf, golf, golf. I never looked at it as a PR exercise. I thought it was all about getting my name on trophies, not getting people to think, "What a nice chap he is." I feel the impression of me was wrong. It was never created, it was purely out of the driven pursuit of winning and trying to be the best. It would be really nice over the next few years to show that I have a different side to me.'

Shadow Ridge is different too, or at least it is in comparison to the other courses in the deserts of the Palm Springs area. This is why it has made such a glorious impact. The story goes that in the first meeting between Nick and his design team, both parties threw down the same magazine, opened it at the same page and pointed to the same picture. So it was Kingston Heath in Australia on which Shadow Ridge was to be based.

As the round continues, you can tell by the way Nick surveys the terrain that this is a course that pleases him. As he points out a small blemish to his designer or explains to me the need for lethal drop-off points around some of the greens, he does so with equally enthusiastic relish.

The bunkering here is an absolute work of art.

on, Nick, hit a draw with a 2-iron," and out would go this draw.'

The golfer in Nick Faldo is still there. I don't suppose it will ever disappear altogether. The chance to reminisce with the six-time major winner about his greatest moments is too good to miss, and he doesn't need much encouragement.

'Or the knockdown shot with a 5-iron on the 15th?' I venture.

'Yup, that was a low fade into a gale and I'd go boom, and there it was. You'd conjure up a shot and go and do it and that's what pisses me off now because I can't do it any more. The little experiments don't come off. I'm way more imaginative and creative at shot making than I've ever been given credit for. This mechanical man bit, I don't know where that came from. Well, I do. It was Leadbetter, the swing changes and the checking of all the positions, but out on the course I'm trying to hit all sorts of fades and draws. My best asset is these fellas.' He holds his hands out towards me. 'I don't think I've been given the credit I deserve for the imagination I've shown.'

'I can remember that fade you hit at Wentworth

'I FEEL THE IMPRESSION OF ME WAS WRONG. IT WAS NEVER CREATED, IT WAS PURELY OUT OF THE DRIVEN PURSUIT OF WINNING AND TRYING TO BE THE BEST.'

from the trees on the right of the 15th in the World Matchplay Championship in 1989,' I say.

'Exactly. There's the guy who can only hit it straight, playing a low cut to about five feet and boom, thank you very much. But it was usually more subtle with me. You'd know Seve was shaping the ball because he'd be in the trees, but I was in the fairway. I'd be holding the ball up with fades and draws and it wouldn't be so obvious. That's why I'd look disappointed sometimes on a shot that worked out well, because I'd be trying to play a draw and it would end up being a fade. You don't get a buzz from that. But I knew that if I really needed it, I could hit the right shot at the right time.'

When we reach the 13th hole, Nick turns his attention back to the course. As he stands on the tee there's something about the make-up of the hole he doesn't like. It's a short par 4 up a small valley with quite heavy bunkering up both sides of the fairway. From the landing area, the hole turns left almost at right angles, leaving a short wedge

or 9-iron to a green nestled round the corner. He doesn't like the trees on the left because he wants to encourage the big hitters to go for the green. He gave orders to have the bunkers made more severe to increase the risk and reward strategy. The logic of it makes sense, and as Nick marches up and down checking yardages, his chief designer scribbles notes.

As far as our match is concerned, Nick is comfortably ahead, but that doesn't seem to matter. He has other things on his mind and I'm quite happy to keep the scorecard in my pocket having made numerous visits to the striking yellow hay into which the lush greenery is set.

'Was there a day or a time when you realized that the edge wasn't there any more?' I ask.

'Do you know, the odd thing about this game is that I won Riviera in 1997 and I won it well. I got into the lead and I stayed there. Guys were having a go and I was just fending them off one by one. Then, just a couple of weeks after that it didn't feel the same any more. It was weird, and

Nick's new course is called Shadow Ridge and it's created a real buzz of excitement in the Palm Desert area. It's easy to see why.

it's been a bit downhill since then.

'It's so hard when you can't perform in the way you know you can. Take Muirfield again. I mean, coming down the 17th in that final round I hit two great shots there: a high draw off the tee, which is definitely not my natural shot, followed by a 4-iron 20 feet left of the stick. That was a perfectionist par 4, and my four at the last was a gem.'

'A 3-iron straight at the pin.'

'I dreamt of that shot, even down to the win. I dreamt that I came to the last hole and I'd have a 3-iron into a right-to-left breeze and I had exactly that shot. That's wacky, eh?'

'You're not having these dreams now then?'

'It's more design dreams now, that or Julia Roberts. Maybe that's it, maybe I should be working on my golf dreams. I've always played my golf as a preparation for the majors. I remember something that Ian Connelly told me once. Ian played a practice round with Gary Player the last time the Open was at Hoylake, in 1967. He said Gary carved it right on the 16th and was in a

terrible lie on the bank, but he went in there and played it. Ian asked him why he bothered, and Gary replied that if he hit it in there on Sunday he wanted to know what it was like. I think that advice has gone into my subconscious.'

I too, like Gary Player, have been practising hacking it out of the rough, so much so that the handshake that comes on the 18th green should, in the context of the match, have occurred a number of holes earlier.

Nick Faldo's relaxed nature on the golf course is now evident on stages far more significant than this. He knows it could be to the detriment of his game, but somehow that doesn't matter any more. 'The business side is kicking into gear and I'm really enjoying trying to develop this company that I have,' he says.

As the shadows lengthen at Shadow Ridge, I leave through the pro shop and notice that the little metal steam train is still there. It hasn't moved and, at $75, I don't expect it to. It will sit there amid the dawn of a new era, in recognition of a past one.

PADRAIG HARRINGTON

It's difficult at any time to regard *A Round With The Tour Pros* as any kind of real work, even if juggling a notebook, a pen and a golf club at the same time requires the sort of hand–eye coordination Harry Houdini was good at. Indeed, it becomes a pleasure when you find yourself in Portugal, at Quinta do Lago, teeing it up against Padraig Harrington. Not only is the sun shining, but my opponent is charm personified. Easy-going, amiable and eager to give everyone a decent time, he pronounces himself up for our match. And as he confirms all the above he never stops smiling that broth-of-a-boy, white-toothed grin that's a trademark underlining to his Wilson visor. I get the feeling that if I ask him to clean my hire car he'll do something about it.

Padraig Harrington is one of Europe's hardest workers, and it's started to pay off in a big way.

One other point. Padraig, you'll notice, is not wearing his visor in the photographs because they had been mislaid in transit and the replacements were lost in the mystery that is the Portuguese postal service. This, rather humiliatingly I felt, seemed to concern Harrington rather more than our match. Still, his degree was in accountancy, so what can you expect?

And so to the first hole, a 380-yard downhiller. Padraig's drive, from a tee several miles behind mine, rockets away to within 120 yards of the green. My ball, too, is blasted off. Sadly, the blasted thing goes into the trees on the left. When my caddie and I get there I decide that in the absence of talent I shall resort to my more natural con game. So with Padraig in earshot I announce

an awesome drive and then conquers this 550-yard hole with a driver off the deck. I can't hit the ball off a peg with an 11° club and he can nail it off the fairway with an 8.5° driver. Life, as ever, is simply not fair. Two played, two down.

It's time for radical action. Sod the clubs, I think, I'm concentrating on the notebook and pen. At least I can't lose them in the rough.

'So Padraig, tell me, what's the main difference between you the pro and you the outstanding Irish amateur?'

His reply is as much of a surprise as the 5-iron I subsequently catch flush. Flush, that is, into a lake on the left.

'I'll tell you what the difference is: I had a much better short game as an amateur,' says this

Watching Padraig's short game is an education in itself, although he admits this part of his game was far better when he was an amateur.

rather grandly to my man that I shall take a 6-iron, knock it out low under the branches and hook it onto the green. Do you know what? I did. Don't ask. I've no idea how I managed it, but Padraig suddenly looked a smidgen less complacent. Or maybe he was still just confused by the absence of that bloody visor. Of course, he holed his birdie putt from 20 feet while I three-putted from 15. I know, I know ... but the green was slippier than a Docklands eel pie and there was nothing I could do about it.

At the 2nd things really go pear-shaped, my attempted drive nosediving into jungle on the left whence I never emerge. Padraig, meanwhile, hits

**I HAD A MUCH BETTER SHORT GAME AS AN AMATEUR. WE USED TO PLAY A LOT OF OUR MATCHES ON HARD LINKS COURSES AND YOU NEEDED TO BE GOOD AROUND THE GREENS ... I JUST DON'T GET THE PRACTICE THESE DAYS.'

Padraig says he gets jittery before a tournament starts, but once the gun goes there is great authority and confidence stamped on his game.

former Irish Open and Closed and Walker Cup champ. 'We used to play a lot of our matches on hard links courses and you needed to be good around the greens, and I was. I'd give my eye-teeth for it today. I just don't get the practice these days. Partly it's the courses we play and partly it's the fact that I'm straighter and a better all-round golfer. I hit more greens now than I did then.'

Three down.

'What else don't you like now as opposed to then? What, for example, do you dislike most about yourself as golfer?'

Padraig grins again, mostly at his caddie David

McNeilly, an Ulsterman who plays a sort of relentlessly Belfast Proddy Baldrick to Padraig's urbane Catholic Dublin-born Blackadder. 'I'll tell you what I wish I could make different. I wish I wouldn't be so negative in the couple of days before a tournament begins. I'm fine once the gun goes, but before that I'm fidgeting about with this and that, convincing myself that I can no longer play the game half decently. I know I'm doing it, but it still drives me mad.'

'Your worst moment on a golf course?'

'On the course it was the way I messed up a great chance of winning the Irish Youths from two up with four to play. I got ahead of myself that

PADRAIG ON ...
THE BEST OF EVERYTHING

DRIVING
I feel I have to pick players in each category whom I've
actually seen close up. So for driving I can't look past
Tiger. He's awesome off the tee. Most other places too.

LONG IRONS
Nick Faldo was a fantastic long-iron player in his prime,
but I also like Bernhard Langer who has such
tremendous control of distance.

SHORT GAME
It's a toss-up between Ollie and Seve because each of
them has such a tremendous variety of shots they can
play. You need technique, obviously, but imagination is
maybe even more important, and those two guys have
that all right.

PUTTING
Difficult. But I tell you what, I'll pick myself if that
doesn't come across too badly. I started putting left
hand below right when my stroke went AWOL before
the European Q-school in 1995 and I've stuck with this
set-up. I'm a decent putter. Certainly, if I had to have
someone to putt for my life from 15 to 25 feet then I'd
do it myself.

MENTAL APPROACH
Bernhard Langer, without doubt. If you welded his
determination and positive approach onto Seve's pure
excitement and intensity, then what a player you'd have.

day and bogeyed three of the remaining holes.
That still burns. Around the course, the worst was
what happened in 2000 at The Belfry. [Blimey.
My last memo to myself was, whatever else you
do, don't mention The Belfry and that scorecard,
and here your man is bringing up the subject
himself.] I actually got to grips with what
happened at The Belfry quite quickly. People say I
handled it well, but what else could I do? It was a
stupid error, something you never think of
happening. Not really. And also in a funny sort of
way it was easier to cope with than if I'd played
in that last round with such a big lead and then
messed up on the course. I don't know if you can
understand that but in a way that would have been

**'THE GREATEST MYTH IN THE GAME IS SWALLOWED BY MOST
AMATEURS WHO BELIEVE THAT TO PLAY THIS GAME HALF
WELL YOU MUST REMAIN PERFECTLY STILL OVER THE BALL.
IT'S NONSENSE.'**

much more damaging to me. I can always go
through life now thinking I would have won that
one even if I never picked up a cheque.'
   We reach the 9th tee, and for those of you still
fascinated by our match, I should mention that I
was five down at this stage which meant there had
been a recovery of sorts. This was due mostly to
Padraig taking pity on me and suggesting
something no one had ever mentioned before: my
right leg was too straight on my backswing and
therefore I couldn't get my weight moving
forward quickly enough. I was hitting it off the
back foot. His remedy was to have me lift my
right heel an inch off the ground. From this
position it's impossible to straighten the back leg
and the right knee kicks in properly. Brilliant.
I win the 9th to get back to four down.
   'I'm not a coach and I never will be,' Padraig
asserts. 'A coach would adapt basic principles to
fit your game. I can't do that. All I can do is tell
you how I play the game and some of the little
tricks I use. We all need someone else to look us
over. You can't do it yourself. Golf is a game of
opposites and it's hard to get your head around
that fact and to work it out. The greatest myth in
the game is swallowed by most amateurs who
believe that to play this game half well you must
remain perfectly still over the ball. It's nonsense.
Watch any pro and you'll see we all move all the

time, we even sway, which you lot think is a big no-no. Yet time and again I see amateurs freezing over the ball, their energy draining away into some sort of trance. From that position it's all but impossible to hit a good shot.'

I find all this fascinating. So fascinating, so invigorating, that I lose the next two holes. Six down, seven to play. But then I re-emerge from my cocoon of journalistic concentration and reinvent myself as a golfer. Gone is the lack of focus and swing that blighted my front nine. In its place is a thing of real beauty. Well, okay, a thing of near competence. But it feels beautiful. After 13 holes I'm back to five down with five to play, then four down, then three, then two.

The small crowd following us has got into this ludicrous match and, crikey, they seem to be on my side, even applauding my exquisite wedge to 12 feet at the long 17th while Padraig can only flop his third 25 feet short. I have the bugger on toast. I'm going to recover from dormy-five down against Padraig Harrington to halve the match and earn gloating rights for the rest of my natural. This thought is echoed loudly and happily by McNeilly, who is already working out how swiftly he can tell the other players and caddies about Padraig's failure to beat a fellow Belfastman with one knee almost missing.

Except that Padraig holes his 25-footer for a birdie, and although I match his birdie four (net) it's all over. Still, 2&1 is better than I could have hoped for half a dozen holes ago. I feel vindicated, slightly elated and, in a sense, the moral victor. No one else, however, notices.

I'm sure he's being totally honest, but a bit of me thinks, 'Yeah, right!' This is because Jack Nicklaus once said the same thing to me and the next morning I couldn't see what he was having for breakfast over the mound of newspapers on his table. Instead of relating this story, however, I ask Padraig about the Ryder Cup and how he thinks it will go this time. He follows the now accepted party line by saying he's sure it will be close and Europe can win if they have a bit of luck and a few putts fall for them and don't for the Americans. Fine, but what about this being payback time for all that idiocy on the 17th in Boston a few years ago? Is he up for it?

'Ah, c'mon,' he answers. 'That's over and done. They've apologized and that's fine. What it did show was that they cared about the Ryder Cup. Maybe they felt that was an important emotion to show because they had taken a lot of stick in the American media beforehand when they said they wanted to be paid in some way for playing. The Ryder Cup is about passion, and sometimes that means people do things they wouldn't normally. That's the excitement of the thing, for goodness' sake. I know that maybe if the boot had been on the other foot then we might have run across a green too. Who knows?'

Our conversation took place before the dreadful events of September 11 and therefore the 2001 match was still on, but at the time I thought what a considered, intelligent response from a decent bloke. It's a pity Padraig Harrington doesn't read articles about him because now he'll never know how much I enjoyed playing with him. Even if he could have become an accountant.

'I ACTUALLY GOT TO GRIPS WITH WHAT HAPPENED AT THE BELFRY QUITE QUICKLY. PEOPLE SAY I HANDLED IT WELL, BUT WHAT ELSE COULD I DO? IT WAS A STUPID ERROR, SOMETHING YOU NEVER THINK OF HAPPENING.'

'I'd have enjoyed writing this up if I'd got the half,' I say to Padraig as we climb towards the final tee.

'It wouldn't have worried me.' He grins. 'I never read what's written about me. Sometimes I look at the pictures but I never read the articles. I lost in the quarter-finals of the British Youths when I was 18 after reading something that upset me so I promised myself I wouldn't be affected like that again.'

PADRAIG'S GEAR

IRONS: Wilson 2-iron through gap wedge. Fat shafts, stiff.

WEDGE: Ping lob wedge (58°)

DRIVER: Ping driver (8.5°)

3-WOOD: Callaway 13° (so nearly a 2-wood in terms of loft)

PUTTER: Odyssey White Hot

PAUL LAWRIE

On 18 July 1999 a modest Scot ranked 159 in the world created one of golf's greatest ever shocks, charging through the mid-field with a great final round which secured him an unexpected spot in a three-man play-off for the Open Championship. Then, blow me down if he didn't go and win the play-off. Minutes later he was standing there clutching the Claret Jug in his cold, damp hands. 'Champion golfer for the year, Paul Lawrie!'

Fast-forward several months and Paul Lawrie is back at Carnoustie to relive a slice of sporting history. It's the first time the champion has been back since his showdown with Justin Leonard and Jean Van de Velde and he admits the experience is 'a bit spooky'. We decided it would be appropriate for me to take on the Open champion over the same four holes that were contested in the play-off.

Before we head out to the 15th tee, however, I sit down with Paul so he can let me in on some of the secrets of his truly astonishing play-off victory.

'Maybe I'm just thick', he grins at me over a Carnoustie bacon roll, 'but I don't often get myself in a position where I think about what's happening. I just don't seem to get carried away with things.'

This self-control must have been tested to the limit at the 1999 Open, when Paul had to wait 90 minutes between signing his card and teeing it up again on the 15th against Leonard and Van de Velde. He spent the time with his coach Adam Hunter, practising victory celebrations. Should it be vigorous air punching in the style of Ballesteros, or a Hale Irwin sprint around the green? Only kidding. Actually he was practising long putts, knowing that in a play-off birdies mean prizes. He was also working hard on what sports psychologist Dr Richard Cox had been telling him for the past three years: think one step at a time and don't let your mind race ahead.

So no nerves at all then, Paul? Well, just a few. 'We got out of the buggy at the 15th tee and Adam said to me, "Remember, these guys are just as nervous as you are." I made sure I looked at Leonard on the tee and I would say he was more nervous than I was. I was quite nervous, but he was really nervous.'

What was his plan for the play-off, though – did he play his opponents, or the holes?

'The conditions were so different from how they

Lawrie's finest hour, coming from nowhere to snatch golf's greatest prize at the Open Championship at Carnoustie in 1999.

were in regular play that my plan went out of the window,' he reveals. 'But yes, I tried to take each hole as it came. At 17 and 18 the situation had changed a little bit, but certainly at 15 and 16 I had to make sure I played the holes.'

All three men were nervous, it was raining hard, and they all hooked their first drives towards the gorse. Paul emerged with a bogey, but still found himself in a tie for the lead with Justin Leonard.

At the 250-yard 16th the Scot reached for his 3-iron (his 7-wood wasn't in the bag at the Open). The hole was to be another scrappy affair. 'The wind was off the right and a little down,' he tells me, 'or pretty much straight across. I hit it in the right bunker, splashed out to about six feet above the hole and missed the putt. But we all ended up making fours.'

None of the trio had yet parred a hole, never mind birdied one. But the 17th was where things started to turn in Paul Lawrie's favour. With the wind a little off the left, he struck two sweet shots to the green and grabbed the initiative. 'It was raining pretty heavily by then and I was just thinking about making par,' he recalls. 'I could have reached the burn with a driver off the tee, so I hit a 2-iron and had 218 yards left. I decided to hit a 4-iron, pitch it short and run it up to the pin. It was a lovely shot.' To ten feet, in fact. 'Jean holed his putt first and I knew I had to follow him in. He gave me the line, it was just a little bit left-to-right. I felt comfortable over the putt and it

'I HAVE NO PROBLEM WITH WINNING. IF PEOPLE DON'T THINK IT WAS A WIN, THAT'S THEIR PROBLEM.'

went right in the middle.'

It's the scenario every player dreams about – taking a one-shot lead down the last in the Open. Having watched both Leonard and Van de Velde splash into the Barry Burn (now known in these parts as Frenchman's Creek) in regulation play, Paul must have been tempted to take an iron off the tee and play it like a par 5. Not so – he hadn't even got beyond thinking about his tee shot.

'All week I had played a 3- or 4-iron off the tee with a 7- or 8-iron second shot. But this time it was into the wind and it was cold and wet and the bunkers weren't in play, so I went with the driver. I picked my target way off in the distance, which I think was the clock on the clubhouse. I was still trying not to get ahead of myself. I was

determined to take it one shot at a time, and not to fall into the trap of thinking it was over before it actually was.'

His drive went down the right side of the fairway, 221 yards from the pin and 194 yards short of the Barry Burn. It didn't give him the easiest line to the flag, but his only goal was to get his second over the water and let it run onto the green. 'I aimed it at the middle of the green and actually pushed it a little bit,' Paul admits. This 'pushed' 4-iron finished four feet from the hole. And it was only then, he says, that it began to dawn on him that he could win the Open. 'It was just amazing, because the crowd started going bananas and the guy who had been looking after me said, "Run!" It was just a fantastic feeling.'

But what about the aftermath, when people cast aspersions on the value of his victory? Didn't all the scepticism bother him?

'I was playing the last few holes, not thinking I had a chance to win the Open, when all of a sudden I'm in a play-off and I play fantastically well. I have no problem with winning. If people don't think it was a win, that's their problem.'

And since the tournament?

'I overheard a comment at the Ryder Cup where someone said, "That's Lawrie – he hasn't won since the Open." People expected me to win straight away. But I feel that if I do what I'm supposed to do with Dr Cox and Adam Hunter, I will go on from here and win two or three tournaments a year. I don't see why I shouldn't.'

So, there you have it. Straight from the horse's mouth. Now to our little battle. The way I see it, I am the favourite. Just as Paul Lawrie believed he held the advantage going into the four-hole play-off for the 1999 Open Championship, I now feel certain that I have the edge over him. For a start, everyone is expecting Paul to win. This makes me the great British underdog, and automatically qualifies me for a generous slice of good luck and the best wishes of every have-a-go five-handicapper who has dreamed of beating a tour pro. Secondly, the unflappable Mr Lawrie (a wee bit smaller than I had expected) has just gone and told me exactly how he did it last time, shot by shot over those momentous four holes. If Paul thinks I'm going to be another play-off pushover, he's got another thought coming. Four holes is the best chance I will ever have to beat a major champion, and although I know I can't outplay him, I reckon that maybe, just maybe, I can outwit him.

Not the club you'd expect to see in an Open champion's hands, but Paul uses his 7-wood to devastating effect.

THE 15TH — 472 YARDS, PAR 4

Most play-offs are sudden death,' Paul says before we tee off. 'You've got to be a bit aggressive and try to get it over with. The Open is different, because with four holes there's a chance that if you make a mistake early on you can get it back.'

I may soon need to bear this in mind.

When we reach the 15th for the start of our play-off replay, I flash Paul a hard stare. He says he did the same at the Open, and saw a very nervous Justin Leonard grimacing back. Unfortunately, today the poker-faced Scot is looking quite relaxed. Damn! Next I try reverse psychology, putting him off by telling him I am super-nervous, and this seems to work. He

drag-hooks his tee shot ten yards left of the fairway, shaving a fair distance off the dogleg. I step up to the tee box. Despite Paul's wise words about taking each hole as it comes, I find that already my mind is blearily focusing on what Paul will do for his second shot, how I'll feel walking up the 18th, and whether it's roast beef or turkey for lunch. So it's probably no surprise when I shunt my 3-wood off to the right.

Paul and I meet again about ten minutes later, up on the green. He has taken one more shot to get here, with a 7-iron; I've taken two. Now I lure him into a false sense of security with an intentional three-putt to give him a one-hole lead (he makes four, I make six). Everything is going to plan. The only thing is, it's not my plan.

THE 16TH – 250 YARDS, PAR 3

The 16th is as long as a motorway, with a green as narrow as a country lane. And most people don't make the trip without breaking down along the way. So when Paul pulls a 7-wood from his bag, it feels a bit like seeing John Wayne draw a little pink pistol instead of a Smith and Wesson. You expect pros to be rather good with their long irons. Aren't 7-woods for sissies?

'I carry a 7-wood every week on tour,' Paul explains. 'It gives me more height than a long iron going into par 5s. But on links courses I carry a 3-iron instead.'

I'm not completely convinced – until Paul's high-flung hands wallop the ball on a surprisingly low trajectory (more like a 4-wood) to pin high, just off the green to the right. Ah well. Instinct

tells me I can get home with a 3-iron, but despite Paul's advice to concentrate on my own game, my logic now goes haywire: 'My opponent is a tour pro, he took a 7-wood; surely I can't possibly make it with a 3-iron.' Needless to say, my 5-wood goes gusting over the back of the green, leaving me with a 15-yard chip back and two putts for a four. Nice bogey.

Paul, on the other hand, chips skilfully out of the fringe to seven feet and then does something that only really good players can. His super-smooth putting stroke, which hardly seems to accelerate at the best of times, nearly doesn't at all. He lets out an 'Oh dear' as the ball leaves the clubface. But in deference to the fact that he is a champion, it wanders up to the hole, has a look in and drops. The hole is halved in three and I remain one down. Oh dear, indeed.

If anyone should know the line on Carnoustie's fearsome finish, it's a man who won the Open here.

Paul has a putting stroke to die for and frankly never looks like he's going to miss much inside 10 feet.

THE 17TH — 459 YARDS, PAR 4

This is where things started to happen for Paul in the Open, and I can only pray that some of the magic rubs off on me. We both hit good drives into the wind (my driver finishes just a few yards behind his 3-wood) and successfully find the perilously small landing area, which seems surrounded by the Barry Burn. Now I prepare to play my psychological trump card. I choke down on a 3-wood to chase a 200-yard shot under the wind – and snap-hook it into the gorse.

After eight seasons on tour, Paul is clearly so put off by the idea that he might have to search for a ball that he promptly balloons his (ahem) 7-wood short and right. He chips up to around ten feet, but for once his silky putting stroke lets him down and

he takes five. I also take five – minutes, that is, to look for my ball, before conceding the loss of the hole and with it the match.

So there it is. I have been out-psyched and outplayed by the Open champion, and it's over almost before it has begun.

And that's the impressive thing about Lawrie. He might not be the best swinger or ball striker you'll see on tour (although he has a putting stroke to die for), but he's obviously very clear about what he has to do. That was evident at both the Open and the Ryder Cup. And that's half the battle when you're up against a field of pros every week, all of them capable of hitting shots and making low scores. It is mental strength and stamina which pay.

So how about double or quits down the last, Paul?

'I CARRY A 7-WOOD EVERY WEEK ON TOUR. IT GIVES ME MORE HEIGHT THAN A LONG IRON GOING INTO PAR 5S. BUT ON LINKS COURSES I CARRY A 3-IRON INSTEAD.'

No trophy or prize money for this win, just a warm handshake from a humbled opponent.

THE 18TH – 487 YARDS, PAR 4

There's no time for 18th-hole euphoria for Paul today, because I've saved my best for last. Once again he opts for his 7-wood off the tee and finds the left of the fairway, opening up the green. True to form, I bat another 3-wood down the right, not far from where Paul finished at the Open.

The second shot to the green is actually much more difficult than I had imagined. The hole is pan flat, you can't see the burn, and without grandstands it's difficult to judge the distance (not that I'm used to judging distances by grandstands, you understand). Paul hits another 7-wood to the front left edge, while I excite the gallery of 30 diehard locals with a high, drawing 3-iron which drifts in over the right bunker, pitches 15 feet short and runs past the hole to the back of the green. This stupendous effort is greeted by silence. They're rooting for the local boy again, I think to myself. He'll be feeling the pressure now, though. However, Paul calmly rolls his long putt up to within five feet and holes out for a four.

Now I'm torn between having a race for the birdie and settling for a safe par. Still undecided, I trundle the putt down and leave a nasty two-foot left-to-righter, which Paul doesn't give me (obviously he's still in Ryder Cup mode). But I pop it in for a half, a round of applause and a comprehensive stuffing at the hands of the Open champion. My opponent is one over after three pars and a bogey. And I'm – well, a few more than that.

Paul smiles, screwing up his face with a more than passing resemblance to Stan Laurel, and holds out a hand. He's won a Carnoustie play-off again, only this time he doesn't look quite so surprised.

Another putt drops, which means it's another play-off victory for Paul, maintaining his 100 per cent Carnoustie record.

AND THAT'S THE IMPRESSIVE THING ABOUT LAWRIE. HE MIGHT NOT BE THE BEST SWINGER OR BALL STRIKER YOU'LL SEE ON TOUR, BUT HE'S OBVIOUSLY VERY CLEAR ABOUT WHAT HE HAS TO DO

PAUL McGINLEY

It was once said of the great American golfer Tom Kite that of all the players in the world, he made the most out of the least talent. A rather back-handed compliment, perhaps, but acknowledgement nonetheless of the fact that a player can reach the pinnacle of his sport by being resourceful and determined. Irishman Paul McGinley is just such a golfer.

The K Club in Ireland is the glorious setting for this match against Paul McGinley, a powerful player maturing and improving with every year on tour.

He is the consummate professional, leaving no stone unturned, no avenue unexplored, in his quest to be the best he can be. In some ways Paul is the antithesis of his close friend and fellow Irishman Darren Clarke. 'Darren has always been a complete natural,' Paul says. 'He's in a different league from me, no question about it. He's number ten in the world, I'm number sixty. But I'm getting there. I'm progressing all the time, and even now I know that on my day I can beat Darren and those players like him.'

There is an element of the hare and the tortoise about this scenario – another observation for which I hope Paul will forgive me. However, in my defence I say this: Tom Kite became a legend of the game, and we all know where the tortoise finished in the race to the winning post.

When we meet, Paul is embroiled in a race of his own, the race for a 2002 Ryder Cup place (which he eventually secured with a victory in the third last qualifying event, the Wales Open). Given the circumstances, a hectic schedule and the seriousness of his goal, I'd expected him to be a tad preoccupied, a little moody and certainly worn out, but not a bit of it. It is a warm, sunny morning, and the Dubliner is displaying a warm and sunny disposition. That's the good news. The bad news becomes evident when he flashes a smile and heads confidently for the 'European Open' tee. It's a wicked smile and it's a serious back tee, one that has me wondering nervously if failing to get the ball past the ladies' marker carries the same penalty in Ireland as it sometimes does in England.

'I'll give you six shots and we'll play for the drinks,' Paul says, before thumping a drive into the distant corner of the dogleg.

After dispatching two shiny new balls, one left into water and the other right into trees – both comfortably past the ladies' tee, though – I'm already checking the bag to see how much ammunition I have left.

'Play a Taylor Made ball and it would have gone straight,' Paul jokes, before completing a comprehensive demolition job on the 1st by rolling in a ten-footer for a birdie three.

This is to be a nine-hole encounter played over the back nine of the K Club's Arnold Palmer-designed parkland estate. It's a course that has received some poor press in the past because of its problems with irrigation, so I've been looking forward to making up my own mind about its worthiness as the appointed venue for the 2005 Ryder Cup. I'd already had a sneak preview thanks to a reconnaissance round with head greenkeeper Gerry Byrne, and can report that the venue has come a long way in a relatively short space of time. 'This has always been a very high-profile development, and some of the criticism it received was probably quite justified,' Byrne told me. 'But a great deal of money has been spent and now it's ... well, I'll leave you to decide that.'

It's majestic. There's no other word for it. Splashes of yellow gorse, huge creaking chestnut trees, sparkling rivers and the sweet scent of pollen in the air offer a wonderful tranquillity that might explain why Tiger Woods is a frequent visitor. The course is now more than a match for the proud Georgian manor at its heart.

The ambience is enhanced by attention to detail. The owner, Dr Michael Smurfit, has decreed that only the old grey tractors with their chimney exhausts and bowl-shaped seats should be seen from the hotel. But it's the quality of the course that stands out for me, because it has so far failed to get the recognition it deserves. In terms of its Ryder Cup potential you cannot fail to be impressed. The Belfry enjoys its fourth hosting of the event in 2002, but it's not a patch on this layout in Kildare. The Belfry has two showpiece holes; the K Club has six or seven. And when Gerry Byrne promised me a course in immaculate condition, he wasn't exaggerating.

Paul beams at me on the 2nd tee. 'Fantastic, isn't it?' I think he's talking about the vista before us, but it may equally be his drive.

'How important is it to you to make Sam's side?' I ask my opponent.

'It's important, but at the same time I can't put too much pressure on myself. I've played Walker Cup and won the World Cup with Padraig Harrington, and I would love to play Ryder Cup – but I know that if I want it too much I'll get in my own way. I've got to be careful of that.'

Paul's progress in his decade as a pro may have been solid rather than spectacular, but he's collected all the credentials to deserve a Ryder Cup place. They include two tour victories, over

A Georgian manor is a magnificent centrepiece at the K Club and is matched by the quality of the golf course, which will play host to the 2005 Ryder Cup.

IT IS A WARM, SUNNY MORNING, AND THE DUBLINER IS DISPLAYING A WARM AND SUNNY DISPOSITION. THAT'S THE GOOD NEWS

PAUL ON ...
THE BEST OF EVERYTHING

DRIVER

Tiger Woods is very long and he's very accurate. I think you could quite easily have him ahead in every category of the game, particularly his driving and putting. The great thing about Tiger is that not only is he the best player in the world, he's also a wonderful ambassador for the sport and we should not forget that. It's amazing when he comes and plays in Europe — he always looks like he has so much in reserve. He is able to win tournaments when he's only firing at 70 or 80 per cent.

IRON PLAY

I think when he's on song there is one player who is better than Tiger with his irons and that's Colin Montgomerie. I don't think anyone knocks the stick out like he does when he's playing well. His feel for distance can be quite extraordinary.

BUNKER PLAY

Tony Johnstone is an absolute magician out of bunkers, and he leaves the rest of us standing. He actually reads the green on bunker shots so that he can curl the ball into the hole. He gets the clubface very open and uses the bounce of the club unbelievably well. He's also brilliant out of all types of sand — deep, shallow, soft or firm.

PUTTING

Tiger again. No one putts as well as him. Padraig Harrington and Mark McNulty are excellent, too. Tiger likes to drill the ball in, which means he has less of the hole to aim at, although he can allow for less break.

PAUL'S PROGRESS IN HIS DECADE AS A PRO MAY HAVE BEEN SOLID RATHER THAN SPECTACULAR, BUT HE'S COLLECTED ALL THE CREDENTIALS TO DESERVE A RYDER CUP PLACE

£1.5 million in prize money and a Walker Cup record which includes the scalps of Phil Mickelson and Bob May. He lives near Darren Clarke in golf's millionaires' row at Sunningdale, has signed up Lee Westwood's coach Pete Cowen and built a personal gym at his home to beef up his fitness. For now, though, Paul is intent on taking one step at a time. Rungs on the ladder, he calls it.

'Darren Clarke was the tour pro here before

Paul is proud to be the touring pro attached to the K Club and it's easy to see why in view of such natural splendour.

you,' I say. 'Do you think you've struggled to step out of his shadow?'

'Have you heard of Sean Kelly and Stephen Roache?' asks Paul. 'Well, Kelly was the Darren Clarke of the Irish cycling world. He was up there in the top bracket and Roache just wasn't in the same league. Then Roache goes and wins the Tour de France. Now Roache is a bigger name.'

'Do you really think this will make a good Ryder Cup venue?' I ask him.

'Listen, I know what a Walker Cup can be like here in Ireland – it was massive. When the Ryder Cup comes you'll have seen nothing like it. I know there was talk of taking it to a traditional club, but the Ryder Cup is big business now and you can't blame the European Tour for using it to best advantage. They have rewarded the Smurfit Group for what it has done for the European Open – rightly so, in my opinion. I'm particularly pleased for Michael because he has a bad back and his doctor has told him he can't play golf any more. Yet he

owns all this. How tough must that be for him?'

I never thought I'd have much sympathy for a man as wealthy as Michael Smurfit, but I guess I was wrong.

The 16th hole proves a turning point in our match. A drive that rebounds backwards off a tree into a water hazard, followed by a slightly scuffed 5-wood, leads to a concession. The only surprise is that it isn't me who's conceding, but Paul. A temporary aberration, which doesn't prove costly for Paul as on the next tee I manage to dispatch my tee shot into the Liffey. And it looks like curtains as Paul lines up a makeable ten-foot putt for a birdie on the last. But his effort runs just

wide of the hole – something that seems to happen to him more times than he would like on tour. He could have won a couple of times already this year if he'd holed putts at the right time.

'I rarely get really hot with the putter,' he explains. 'Other players have spates of 36 holes when they hole everything. Getting the right pace in your putts is essential, and that's where I've had to work hard. You should aim to get it 18 inches past the hole.'

My tricky downhill eight-footer would have no trouble going a foot and a half past were I given an opportunity to miss it. Paul spares me the trouble.

'Peter, pick that up and we'll have a half in the tradition of Jack Nicklaus and Tony Jacklin,' he says with a typically Irish twinkle in his eye.

I laugh. 'You see, you're thinking Ryder Cup all the time.'

'Maybe, but if I do that at the Belfry they'll have me swinging from the yardarm!'

Paul finds the water hazard on the par-4 16th, on course owner Michael Smurfit's favourite hole.

PAUL'S GEAR

I chose the 360 driver from Taylor Made's 300 series because it was so easy to use. I know the head is pretty big, but I get good distance and I feel very confident with it. I started using the irons in January and have not looked back since. I think I'm up to fifth on greens in regulation now, which just about says it all really. The only equipment change I'll be making now is switching to the new Taylor Made ball when it comes out.

DRIVER: Taylor Made 360. It has 10.5° of loft, bent from 10°, and it's 44 inches long. The shaft is a UST with a stiff tip.

3-WOOD: Taylor Made Super Steel with 14° loft and a Graffalloy X shaft. It's 42 inches long.

4-WOOD: Taylor Made Super Steel which has been bent to a 5-wood loft of 17°. It's 41 inches long with an Aldila shaft.

IRONS: Taylor Made 360s. They all have a 62 grip size with Golf Pride Green Victory grips and they're all 1° flat.

SAND-WEDGE: Cleveland 485. I've changed the loft from 56° to 54° so that it fits between my wedge and lob-wedge.

LOB-WEDGE: Taylor Made Tour 61. The loft is 59° and it has 5° of bounce.

PUTTER: Ping Myday, 33 inches long.

PETER ALLISS

A cold and murky morning greets me at the Hindhead Golf Club, and I'm worried. I have come to Surrey to cross irons with Peter Alliss, and the great man has already said he might not play if it rains. These days it's whispered that his soundbites are far more piercing than his iron play, and his game is not what it once was; he's been the king of TV golf for 25 years, famous for his on-course chats with Brucie and Tarby, but it's rumoured that he can't hit a ball any more. Deep down I'm concerned this may all be bluff. After all, this chap was eight times a Ryder Cup player and finished in the top twenty at the Open Championship eleven times. I just hope I'm not in for a St Valentine's Day massacre.

Peter gleefully points to the author's ball, which has found a nasty spot in the wet, claggy heather lining the fairway.

We meet over coffee, and the doyen of TV commentators is brutally honest about the state of his own game. Peter admits he's no Gary Player, saying, 'I'm old and fat.' He even lets on that he had some sneaky practice the previous afternoon – and played terribly. So can I expect a smother into a bush off the 1st tee?

Happily, no. Peter's ball feels the meat of his driver and careers away down the fairway into the trolley wheels of the group in front. He waves a conciliatory hand, and the player pulling those clubs waves back – impressed, not angry.

Then I step up. I can't blame it on nerves, because I'm already at ease in Peter's fatherly presence, but my driver catches the top quarter of the ball and it bounds apologetically into the heather just 100 yards ahead. At least it was a straight knobble. Things gets worse. My 9-iron rescue attempt scampers ferret-like through the woody stems for all of eight yards, and the next one tiptoes over the beastly stuff but still finishes just short of the fairway. Three shots down, 220 yards to go to the green. I am reddening around the gills by now, but the old master seems to love it. 'It happened to every opponent I ever faced in the Ryder Cup,' he quips.

PETER ON ... THE BASICS

My father Percy used to say, 'Golf is a simple game made complicated by ourselves.' Get a grip that works, aim and line up properly and you're there. Take it back and doddle it. Despite that, there is room for some quirks. Look at Lee Trevino – he was a genius.

Age has shortened Peter's swing to barely half the length of his heyday (left), but good hand-eye skills make for tidy ball-striking.

Poor putting was Peter's Achilles heel. His car registration plate now bears the letters PUTT 3.

As if a double against an easy par isn't a bad enough start, the heavens now decide to open. Thankfully, there's no deterring my opponent now. We continue, and unfortunately so does my dismal golf. Peter, meanwhile, diplomatically ignores my scramblings and sets about punching a workmanlike wood close to the green.

Peter would be the first to admit that his style is not pretty any more. He picks up the club steeply and with alacrity, stopping way short of parallel, and then uses his hand—eye coordination to great effect through the ball. It makes for solid striking. He hits it low and straight, and never misses a fairway all day. For a chap whose annual rounds of golf are outnumbered by the clubs at which he's an honorary member – around 20 compared with 32 – he is a tidy performer.

PETER ON ... CHIPPING

I was taught by Ken Bousfield. I use a long, slow swing so the ball comes off the face softly and releases to the hole. There is no fizz with it like some of today's players. I find it easier to judge that way. Just play it confidently and your swing makes the ball come off delicately.

But why does he play so little golf? 'I made a decision after the 1974 Open at Lytham. I was putting poorly, I was 43, and frankly I'd had enough. I'd been a pro since I was 15. Besides, TV was just starting to happen.' Peter Alliss had the yips before anyone had even thought of a name for them. His putting problems began at Augusta in 1967. 'I had a few invitations but only went twice, which seems sacrilegious now. But people forget how far away it was, and the money wasn't great – about $400 if you got to the last two days. And there, waiting for you, were Ben Hogan, Sam Snead, Jimmy Demaret, Uncle Tom Cobley and all. The chance of doing well was remote.

'In the second round I was out in 36 and doing all right. From the front of the 11th green I putted up to four feet. Then I just went "Psssch" and the ball was 15 feet past, and then 10 feet past. Gene Littler said to me, "What the hell are you doing?" I just said, "I don't know." It could have been seven or eight putts. I may even have put down a wrong score – it was a blur. I have the greatest admiration for Bernhard Langer, who has

PETER ON ... PUTTING STYLES

I don't advocate any one method. You can be an Olázabal who looks up seven or eight times, or a Davis Love who looks once and goes – it doesn't matter as long as it suits you. You just have to be ready. Having said that, I think Davis Love could have won $50 million if he didn't putt the way he does.

come back from the yips two or three times.'

I look out for this Achilles heel on the 3rd when Peter faces a tricky eight-footer, but his short stabby action prods the ball home nonchalantly. It's ironic, because moments earlier he told me his chipping has always been good – and then proceeded to fluff a nasty one off a delicate muddy lie into sand. It leaves me one down after three.

You can tell Peter gets agitated with today's players for taking five hours to get round and forever studying yardage books and every inch of

'I MADE A DECISION AFTER THE 1974 OPEN AT LYTHAM.
I WAS PUTTING POORLY, I WAS 43, AND FRANKLY I'D HAD
ENOUGH. I'D BEEN A PRO SINCE I WAS 15. BESIDES,
TV WAS JUST STARTING TO HAPPEN.'

a putt. He is brisk about his business. No fuss, no dithering. Step up and go.

The skies are ever more sinister as we stroll down the chute of the par-5 4th, but he seems to be in good spirits. He's keen to talk, and whether you agree with his opinions or not, he is brilliant value. Partly it's because he can draw from such rich exposure to the legends and club life, but it's

We escape relatively unscathed from Hindhead's signature hole, the 153-yard Devil's Punchbowl with its 70-foot drop, but finally I am put out of my misery by a curling 12-footer for a two on the temporary green at the 8th. It has been simple yet effective stuff from the man who used to play his TV friendlies with the likes of Sir Douglas Bader, Ted Dexter, Eric Sykes, Val Doonican and Dame Kiri Te Kanawa.

He has been polite and astute, quietly pleased, I think, that he's dispelled any thoughts either of us may have entertained that he struggles on the course. The sharpness and firecracker striking of a honed tour pro may not be there any more, but Alliss knows exactly what he's doing. We shake hands on the 9th and he turns theatrically to the photographer, just as if a TV producer had directed him to.

It has been a day to remember. I've listened and wondered at one of golf's great characters, while my golf wilted in the gathering gloom. We retire to the dining room, where I know the match will be fairer. When it comes to good eating, we're both off scratch!

PETER ON ... COURSE DESIGN

There has never been a great course built without two major ingredients: a nice piece of ground and money. Give anyone 150 acres of flat clay and ask them to build a great course — you can't do it. The pros used to be the architects — Vardon, Braid, Taylor. Then amateurs like Colt, Alison and Mackenzie came along. They were geniuses. There was a stretch when hardly any professionals were involved. But now it has turned full circle and the pros are all the rage. Ask someone what they plan to do after they retire and they'll either say they are waiting to turn 50 so they can make their second fortune, or go into course design. Half of them don't know how to pull on a pair of wellingtons!

also to do with his delivery — that barrelling voice; deep, authoritative and mellifluous. We talk about political correctness: 'It's crept into my life now, and I can't be honest while commentating.' Single-sex clubs: 'If anyone wants to have an all-male or -female club, fine.' Money in sport: 'It's ridiculous — the bubble will burst.' He may be a traditionalist, but his words are passionate and wise.

A grey day is made bright by Peter's colourful stories and a voice you could happily listen to all day long.

PETER JACOBSEN

Peter Jacobsen is about as far removed from your typical Joe Pro as it's possible to be. Aside from being a fine golfer, with two Ryder Cup appearances under his belt and six US Tour victories, he has a reputation for being a joker, entertainer, raconteur, all-round good egg – whichever way you want to put it, he's a bit of a character. So understandably I'm pretty excited about the prospect of a friendly game with the man.

Our match is scheduled for a course Peter and business partner Jim Hardy designed, Blackhorse Golf Club, which is a 30-minute drive from downtown Houston. As I soon discover, this is a public course, Jim, but not as we know it. There are superb and immaculate practice facilities: a massive range and short-game area. There is a huge, well-appointed pro shop. Through the adjoining corridor is a bar and restaurant called Jake's (Peter's nickname) where the walls are adorned with tons of memorabilia celebrating Peter's golfing and musical achievements. Peter used to play in a band called Jake, Trout and the Flounders with fellow tour pros Payne Stewart, Larry Rinker and Mark Lye. The group hasn't performed since Payne's death in 1999.

I spot Peter pulling up in the car park and go out to meet him. He has the warmest of greetings for me and the firmest of handshakes. He is bigger than I was expecting – 6ft 3in and heavily built.

We head over to the practice ground for the obligatory pre-round warm-up. It turns out that Peter's golf course design partner Jim Hardy is here too. Jim is a former tour pro and something of a legend in the teaching world, a man who has studied first-hand all the greats from Ben Hogan to Tiger Woods, including everyone in between. We shake hands and Jim casts a glance at Peter hitting 6-irons, then looks at me and says, 'You're looking at one of the best golf swings in the world here.'

It's kind of Jim to point out that fact to me, but I'm well aware what I'm up against. I'm reminded of an occasion many moons ago, watching a tournament on television and hearing a commentator describe Peter's swing as 'not very natural, a bit mechanical', or something to that effect. 'What utter cobblers' is the thought that strikes me as I play the first few holes with Peter. He looks like he was born to swing a golf club. His method is enviably simple. He takes the club back

In typically jocular fashion, Peter celebrates holing a birdie putt and the lengthening of his advantage in this game by yet another shot.

Peter chokes down on the grip for chip shots, his right hand actually touching the metal on the shaft, which enhances his control of the club head.

deliberately, very smoothly, making a lovely shoulder turn without the club actually reaching horizontal at the top. As he makes his downswing, he just seems to lean into impact, applying a 220lb punch into the back of the ball, which obligingly pings off into the distance on a pleasing trajectory. It's very much under control. I doubt he's ever lost balance hitting a golf shot in his life.

We're playing from the tees ominously described on the scorecard as 'Big Jake', and a closer look at the yardages confirms my worst fears. The opening set – 411, 444, 459 and 228 – are not the sort of numbers I'm either familiar or comfortable with. Peter hits all four greens in regulation and two-putts for a safe par on each.

Already he is hilarious company, having both me and our photographer in stitches. He is also a very thoughtful person, willing to talk on a variety of

personal issues from his friendship with Payne Stewart to the pressures of balancing a career with family life. He seems to have a great perspective on life. He's seen the mistakes others have made and successfully avoided making those mistakes himself. 'In playing the tour,' he explains, 'your life revolves around golf. You think about what food you eat, you practise, you keep in shape, you work on your mind, every aspect of your life is geared to golf. If you're not careful it can affect your family life. I've seen players go through very messy divorces because of that and I wanted to make sure it didn't happen to me. Don't get me wrong, I've always been serious about winning golf tournaments, but I wanted to make sure I had some fun too. I never wanted to get to the point where golf was so important to me that it was everything in my life.'

Peter pauses long enough to caress a drive down

PETER ON ... CHIPPING: ALMOST GRIP THE METAL TO GET GREAT FEEL

One of the things I think is important about a short pitch is to grip right down on the club. For one thing, this increases your feel for the shot. More importantly, though, it effectively shortens your swing arc so you can be a little more positive and accelerate the clubhead through the ball without the fear of overshooting the target. I find that the tendency for a lot of average players is to grip the club long, then they make too long a swing and have to decelerate into the ball. Sometimes you can catch it fat, other times you might skull it over the green. It's tough to get it right when your swing is so long for such a short shot. So try playing it like this. Grip down the club so your right hand is virtually on the steel of the shaft. Now go ahead and hit the shot. You'll automatically have a shorter arc, so your swing feels more compact. You will also get more speed through the ball, which is what you want even though it's a short shot. Payne Stewart played shots in this fashion all the time, and believe me, he was a fantastic wedge player.

PETER ON ...
THE BEST OF EVERYTHING

DRIVING

In his prime Greg Norman was the best driver I've ever seen. People don't give him enough credit for being the great player he was. He was a brilliant driver of the golf ball. Not incredibly long, but very accurate and very good under the gun. Maybe Tiger has broken the mould with driving recently, because he's incredibly long and incredibly straight.

FAIRWAY WOODS

Mike Reid. They call him 'Radar'. He was always a short hitter, but he was very accurate with his fairway woods. He could hit a 3-wood into whichever side of the fairway he needed to give himself the best line into the flag for a wedge shot, better than anyone else in the game. And he could hit fairway woods closer to the hole than anyone I've ever seen.

LONG IRONS

I'd nominate Tom Weiskopf. I played with Tom in my early years on tour and I was so impressed with how high and straight he hit his long irons. I'd say John Daly is a close second, though. He hits incredibly high and incredibly soft long irons. He's one of the greatest natural swingers I've ever seen play the game.

MID IRONS

Johnny Miller. Again, I played a lot with him in the early part of my career. I have great respect and admiration for Johnny as a player and also as a person. I think he has probably kept his life in better perspective than anyone else on tour. He really is one of the most well-rounded people I've ever met out here.

CHIPPING

Seve, obviously. I'd also say Craig Stadler. He grips down at the bottom of the grip and he has fabulous touch. He's great around the greens.

PUTTING

I love to watch Tiger play because to my mind he's the greatest putter I've ever seen. I think Tiger is better even than Ben Crenshaw. Ben has a magical stroke, long and flowing, with phenomenal rhythm. Tiger sets up textbook solid, his shoulders, hips, knees, eyeline all perfectly square. His hands are perfect on the grip, too. And he makes a dead-perfect stroke. If you're looking for someone from whom to learn how to play, Tiger is where you start and stop! Tom Watson when he was winning was an amazing putter too. When you watched him have an eight-foot putt to win a tournament, you knew he was going to make the putt. He knew he was going to make the putt. Everybody watching knew he was going to make the putt. So how the heck was he going to miss it!

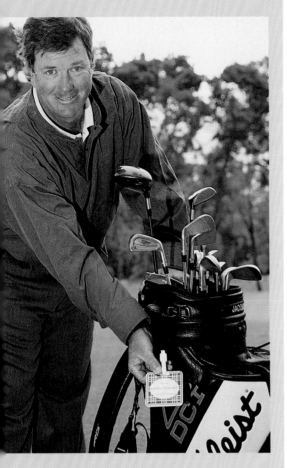

PETER'S GEAR

DRIVER: 9.5°, Titleist 975J, True Temper X-Flex.

3-WOOD: 13.5°, Titleist 975F, True Temper X-Flex.

IRONS: 2-iron through pitching-wedge, Titleist 990b, S300 True Temper Dynamic Gold.

WEDGES: Bob Vokey design, 56° and 62°.

PUTTER: Scotty Cameron, Laguna mid-slant tour platinum.

BALL: Titleist Pro VI.

BAG TAG: Payne Stewart would have been the defending champion at two tournaments had he lived to play in the 2000 US Open at Pebble Beach — he'd won the AT&T Pro Am in 1999 and, of course, the US Open at Pinehurst. So when we got to Pebble Beach they gave these tags to every competitor and I've kept it on my bag. I've had people offer to buy it off me, but I'll always keep it. I like it. It reminds me of an old friend.

THIS MAN'S ONLY MAJOR WIN WAS THE US OPEN ... IN THE MOVIE TIN CUP. BUT THERE ARE MORE WAYS TO WIN IN LIFE THAN BY COLLECTING SILVERWARE

the middle of the 5th fairway, then goes on.

'I remember Nick Faldo being quoted in a magazine once that he would hate to look back on his career and say to himself, "I could have won more majors if I hadn't had so much fun." Nick is a great friend of mine, but I have to say I'm the opposite of that. Sure I want to win tournaments, but I want to have fun. I've been blessed with an ability to play golf. Why not take advantage of that and enjoy it?'

Having fun isn't what prevented Peter winning more tournaments, rather a slight weakness on the greens. As he explains to me on the way round, this is hardly surprising when you learn of his formative years in the game. 'My father taught me how to play golf, but he wasn't a good putter, so he didn't teach that part of the game to me. We'd go out and play 18 holes in two hours and hit three or four balls into each green, then pick 'em up and go to the next tee. That was my development as a player, which is why I don't think I developed the ability to putt like some of my contemporaries. When you're young putting becomes instinctive and I think some of that stays with you. I didn't have that.'

Of course, all things are relative. Peter wouldn't have won six tournaments, more than $6 million and been on tour for a quarter of a century if he didn't know how to get the ball in the hole when he needed to. It's just been a bit on and off, as he admits. 'I've had moments when I've putted great, but there have also been times when I've lost confidence. In a way it's similar to Bernhard Langer. No one in their right mind would say Bernhard is a bad putter, but he's had spells when he's lost confidence. I mean, he's had the yips, but today he's still a tremendous putter.'

For Peter to have a bout of no-confidence on the greens today may be stretching his hospitality a tad. Considering the fact that he designed the course, it's hardly surprising he's reading the greens rather well. And his sure-handed stroke is causing the ball to threaten the hole with a regularity I find rather worrying. He slots home a putt for birdie on the par-5 5th, then eases a 6-iron to 12 feet at the next and cans that for a birdie-two.

We make the turn with only two shots in it, a fact Peter greets with a mixture of mild surprise and amusement. Like a cat playing with a hapless mouse, he birdies the 10th while I make a bogey and the gap is stretched to four. The mouse bites back, though, with a welcome birdie at the 11th. Peter congratulates me heartily, then, as we walk off the green, uses his superior weight advantage to give me a hefty shove into a deep greenside bunker.

It's long since been obvious to me during the course of this round that Peter is a class act and can still really play the game, which makes his comparatively meagre tournament schedule frankly a little surprising. But this has been a conscious move on his part over a number of years. 'When I turned 40, which was seven years ago, my wife said to me, "Look, we've been doing this for a long time, maybe you should cut your schedule down and spend more time at home with the kids." That's what I did, and I'm glad I did it. I didn't want to be dependent on making four-footers to feed my family. I turned some of my attention to some business interests which have been good for me.' Those business interests include Jacobsen/Hardy Golf Course Design, the team responsible for the course we're playing today; a turf equipment distribution business which Peter set up with his brother; and a tournament management operations and marketing company. 'I wanted to make sure there was life after golf. I've seen a lot of golfers who were successful, won many tournaments all over the world, then all of a sudden when they don't play as well they become bitter, hostile and angry with the world. I think that's because they make their world too shallow.'

Unlike my divots. Playing in the company of the course's creator, I'm almost ashamed at the chunk of earth I manage to shift with my approach to the 14th. A bogey-five is my punishment. When Peter plays an exquisite bunker shot to a couple of inches on the 15th (he was second in the US Tour's sand save percentages in 2000) the ensuing tap-in birdie-four pretty much seals my fate in this match. There's just enough time for Peter to make his sixth birdie of the day – courtesy of a solid drive, delicate pitch to six feet and safe putt – then two pars to finish with a round of 67. Five under par, with just one bogey after an uncharacteristically errant drive way back on the 8th hole, is a fair reflection on the consistency of his stroke making.

On a long course, in the face of class opposition, I've done rather better than I thought I would. Which to my surprise is how Peter feels about his golf career. As we share a beer and a burger in Jake's bar, he talks candidly about his life. 'Oh, I've

Peter has a wonderfully simple technique and maximises the natural power in his 6ft 3in frame to give the ball a solid hit.

'SURE I WANT TO WIN TOURNAMENTS, BUT I WANT TO HAVE FUN. I'VE BEEN BLESSED WITH AN ABILITY TO PLAY GOLF. WHY NOT TAKE ADVANTAGE OF THAT AND ENJOY IT?'

definitely done better than I thought I would,' he admits. 'When I turned professional I just hoped to be able to get my card and play on the tour, because I loved golf. Don't forget, when I started in 1976 pro golf was an unbelievable way to make money, but only if you won tournaments. When I look back on my 25 years on tour and see what I've accomplished, where I've travelled to, the people I've met and the life I've been able to build for myself, it's way beyond my wildest dreams. That's why if I never hole another four-footer, never hit another quality shot, I won't care. I've hit plenty, more than my fair share, in fact. And I don't expect to be able to do that every day. I'm not a Tiger Woods type of player, never have been. But that's okay. I am who I am and I'm happy with what I've achieved. If I continue on the Seniors Tour and play well out there, so much the better. It's another chapter in my life that I'm really looking forward to.'

This man's only major win was the US Open … in the movie *Tin Cup*. But there are more ways to win in life than by collecting silverware, and in that sense I get the impression Peter's done rather well for himself. No wonder he's so jolly.

PETER THOMSON

My early morning tee-off with the five-time Open champion Peter Thomson is fast approaching. We are to play at the Duke's Course in St Andrews, a layout Thomson designed himself – so, as you may imagine, knobbling my first few shots along the ground is not top of my wish list.

Even at 70 there is much to admire about Peter Thomson's game, which in his heyday won him five Open Championships.

I decide to stroll up to the practice ground and hit a few looseners. On the way out of the clubhouse, I bump into Thomson arriving.

'I'm off to hit a few balls,' I say to him.

'That's a bit unsporting, isn't it?' He smiles. 'You can't do that. Come and have a coffee with me.'

It would be rude to refuse.

Five minutes before our tee time we're still chatting in the lounge, admiring the wonderful view across the course to the town of St Andrews and along the east coast to Carnoustie. Not even in my golf shoes yet, I'm flouting every warm-up rule I've ever learned. Steve Toon, Duke's Course secretary, comes in and politely suggests we make our way to the tee. My opponent takes a final gulp of coffee and off we go.

Arriving on the 1st tee I notice that Peter is still in his street shoes. He's not wearing a glove either (a legacy of copying his boyhood hero Ben Hogan), and his golf bag is pencil thin, an old-fashioned leather model with a solitary pocket for balls and a small leather tag with his name and address showing through the plastic window. In the bag are half a dozen irons, a driver, a 3-wood and a putter. This minimalist approach typifies the way he has always played the game, and he's clearly not about to change now. Peter casually walks onto the tee with his driver and, after a few waggles of the club, smacks the ball 240 yards down the middle of the fairway.

'Follow that,' he says to me with a smile. Right-ho, thanks Peter!

Thankfully, I hit a good one, and after a couple of shots we are both within 30 yards of the pin, one of Peter's trademark pot bunkers eliminating the chip-and-run option. He plays first, very tidily, and the ball just slips past the hole to within six feet. My untidy effort finishes 30 feet away. I miss. Peter holes for birdie. That'll be one down after one, then.

I discover that Peter is well practised in the art of ... well, not practising. When he was playing tournament golf, practice balls were not provided like they are now. 'You had to carry your own,' he recalls, 'and I don't think any of us had more than a dozen. It was just a matter of having a bit of gentle warm-up before your round, and the caddie would go and pick them up. If you asked him to go twice you got a very dirty look, so you didn't tend to ask!'

Until today I'd never met Peter Thomson, never even seen footage of him hitting a shot. But having talked to John Jacobs, who spent time with the Aussie in his heyday, I felt like I knew a bit about his golf. Temperament was his greatest strength. I'd heard that when it came to the last few holes of an Open Championship, Thomson would be the calmest person on the course – and that included the spectators. 'That's probably true,' he admits now. 'I used to enjoy it. When you enjoy being in contention and you're not afraid, it obviously helps. If I wasn't near winning coming into the last round I'd really lose interest. Couldn't be bothered, to tell you the truth. But if I got a sniff of winning, that's what lifted me – like sniffing glue!'

Blimey – addicted to winning. It must have been heady stuff. Happily, he never had to endure long periods of withdrawal. His record in the Open is astounding. From 1951, when he was 20, it reads like this: 6th, 2nd, 2nd, 1st, 1st, 1st, 2nd,

Peter putts from off the green, the ball coming to rest only 12 inches from the hole. He says it's one of the most under-exploited shots in golf.

'ONE OF THE THINGS ABOUT GOLF TODAY IS THIS OBSESSION WITH THE SAND-WEDGE. PLAYERS WANT TO USE IT EVERYWHERE. I SAY KEEP THE BALL ON THE GROUND WHENEVER YOU CAN.'

PETER ON ...
PLAYING 'SHOTGUN' TACTICS

I'm always amazed how players are so easily drawn into bunkers, even though there might be half an acre of green to the side. Some golfers just don't have the brains to hit it there. Whenever I teach youngsters these days, I tell them a lesson I learned from a young age. Next time you're on the practice ground, get 20 balls and aim at a flag with a short to medium iron. Try to put every shot close to the flag. When you've finished, walk down there and look at your results. Even if you're a good player, the ring of balls is probably 30 feet wide. That's your shotgun pattern, if you like, and what you should do is apply that to actual situations on the course. By that I mean you need to make sure you aim in such a way that your whole pattern will fit onto the green — which usually means aiming at the middle of the green. Some shots will finish close, others will be wide, but they'll probably still be on the green and that's no bad thing.

I STUDY HIS PRE-SHOT ROUTINE, A PART OF HIS GAME WHICH CAN SCARCELY HAVE CHANGED IN HALF A CENTURY. YARDAGES MEAN NOTHING, THAT MUCH IS OBVIOUS

1st, 23rd, 9th, 7th, 6th, 5th, 24th, 1st, 8th, 8th. Even into the 1970s he was still notching up top-ten finishes. Did he feel invincible in the Open, as Tiger seems to in every tournament? 'Yes, I went every year thinking that I'd win,' he admits. 'It was the peak of the season for me and I thought a lot about it. I really enjoyed winning my championships. The fact there was a lot less money to be won made it very different from today. I sometimes joke that the reason I won five times was that the prize money was so small. It ran out so quickly! These days, if you win one you're set up for life.'

Aside from his Open record, Peter was good enough to triumph wherever and whenever he turned up. On one occasion he flew over to England for a tournament, arrived too late to fit in a practice round, yet still won by 15 shots. And his CV contains just about every national Open

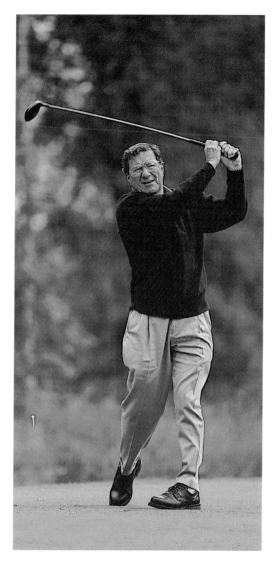

At the age of 70 Peter has retained much of the crisp ball striking and straight hitting that made him such a formidable player in his heyday.

words to say about my 'common sense' on the course, but over these early holes I find myself more preoccupied with watching him play. At the age of 70 he retains the calm self-assurance of his prime – even if the golf ball doesn't always behave quite as it used to. I make a mental note that I must above all try to convey the sheer simplicity of Peter Thomson's game.

I can't help thinking how much every club golfer would learn if they could only be here to watch him now. He plays very briskly, with no messing about, so that I struggle to find time between shots to take the notes I will need to write this story. I study his pre-shot routine, a part of his game which can scarcely have changed in half a century. Yardages mean nothing, that much is obvious. Thomson has always judged distance entirely by eye, and that's the way he still plays.

Just before he addresses the ball, he waggles the club back and forth in mid-air, his gaze fixed on the target. Within five seconds of the club coming to rest behind the ball, the swing is underway, smoothly and with no hint of hurry. It's a treat to watch, and I'm intrigued to get as many of his thoughts on the swing as possible. I find his simple approach is more than skin deep.

'Aiming was everything in my game. It still is,' he says. 'Once I'm set up, I just draw the club back and hit it.'

When you're preparing to play a shot, what are you thinking about then?

'I imagine what it will feel like as I strike the ball

played in Europe in the 1950s and 1960s. When he played the fledgling US Seniors Tour in the mid-1980s, he cleaned up.

No one was better than Peter at plotting a trouble-free path round the golf course.

'I never liked missing fairways,' he says when I remark on his incredibly straight hitting, 'so I tried to make damn sure I didn't.' He compares teeing off to getting your first serve in on the tennis court. 'Above all, get the ball in play,' he urges. What about shaping the ball off the tee? 'I never used to do that,' he says. 'I don't think anyone else did either, to be honest. That's just making a simple thing more difficult, and what's the sense in that? Shooting good scores is all about eliminating mistakes. I didn't call it course management, like they do today. It was just common sense.'

Later in the round Peter will have a few strong

PETER ON...
NICKLAUS, HOGAN AND SNEAD

Jack Nicklaus was the greatest performer, no question. You only have to look at his record. Sam Snead was the most gifted I've seen. The way he played was so natural. But Ben Hogan is the best player of all time. It was a great education to me, watching him when I was a young man. I could see in him things I've never seen since. He had what you might call a manufactured method, a very quick tempo and a tremendous lateral sway that didn't come out in photographs. What never gets written about is the fact that his backswing was so long the shaft of the club would hit him on the back of the neck. That was always amazing to me. His ball striking was phenomenal, though. He'd play all week and not mishit a shot. He may have missed the target a bit, misjudging the wind or whatever, but he'd never mishit a shot. Hogan wasn't a very eloquent man so you never got much conversation from him on the course, but he was very considerate to play with. He didn't strut the stage. Once he'd played his shot he got out of the way.

– that feeling in my hands when I make contact.'

Several times on the fairway I watch the ball and not his swing. His strike is crisp and clean. 'I like to squeeze the ball out, trap it. That's the way I have always played. I don't try to pick it off the top.'

On the 4th, Peter's approach shot comes to rest some ten yards off the green in a tricky spot. To my surprise, out comes the putter. He nudges the ball up to within a foot of the flag. Peter feels this is one of the game's most under-exploited shots, not because he's a poor chipper (he's anything but; he still has nice touch) but because it makes sense. 'One of the things about golf today is this obsession with the sand-wedge. Players want to use it everywhere. I say keep the ball on the ground whenever you can. In the right situation it's easier to judge.'

Peter's gift for shot selection is making it hard

IN THE BAG ARE HALF A DOZEN IRONS, A DRIVER, A 3-WOOD AND A PUTTER. THIS MINIMALIST APPROACH TYPIFIES THE WAY HE HAS ALWAYS PLAYED THE GAME

for me to peg back an early deficit, and his putting isn't helping matters either. On the 8th he holes a 20-footer for par and chooses this seemingly inapposite moment to tell me that he has never been a great putter. 'Bobby Locke was the best in my day. He wasn't in the same class as some of the great putters today, but he was better than everyone else, partly because virtually no one was a good putter back then. You didn't really try to be. I know that sounds funny, but when you got on the green it was almost like you were supposed to take two putts. You never lined up a putt from 35 feet like everyone does now. That's partly why the game was played so quickly.'

At the 11th, the longest hole on the course, I discover Peter hasn't forgotten how to play the tough shots. After yet another drive down the middle he takes a quick look at the lie of the ball on the fairway and reaches for his driver. 'Let's have a go at this,' he says, and hits a carbon copy of his drive, the ball struck as pure as Highland spring water. He then plays a cute running pitch shot from 60 yards with a 9-iron, but the birdie putt stays out.

I'm starting to grow in confidence, partly thanks to Peter's advice after I mishit an iron shot a few holes back. 'You're thinking too much

PETER ON ...
RHYTHM, NORMAN AND FALDO

Rhythm is such an important aspect of the golf swing. It can easily change with your mood. If you feel excited and het-up you'll swing too quickly and jerkily. If you're relaxed and happy, which is the way I always played, you'll swing smoothly. I think I was born with that temperament, though. Everyone's different. You couldn't get a better example of the importance of rhythm than the two classic confrontations between Nick Faldo and Greg Norman, first at St Andrews in 1990 and then at Augusta in 1996. There was someone with wonderful rhythm and someone with none. The scores reflected that difference. In my opinion Greg never understood rhythm. He was too tight over the ball. Faldo always had great rhythm. He'd stand over the ball, have a couple of waggles and away he went.

about your swing,' he said. 'I can tell from the way you're standing over the ball too long. Forget your swing, you're stuck with it. Just keep a good rhythm and think of the bat hitting the ball.'

For the first time in the round my 'bat' starts making proper contact. I write down Peter's tip on the back of the scorecard. I'll make sure I don't forget that one. Peter's no miracle worker, though, and my errant tee shot on the 12th finishes in the right-hand bunker – right in a neat size-10 footprint. Peter's unsympathetic reaction makes me laugh, but it stems from the fact that in his prime the sand was seldom raked. You could get almost any lie. 'You expected it,' he recalls. 'If you put your ball in the sand you copped what you got. It was tough.' Perhaps this explains why he learned to hit the ball so straight.

The match remains close, but in truth I hardly ever look like getting on even terms. Not until the par-5 15th, that is. I hit a 3-wood to six feet. Peter tracks his usual neat path up the centre of the fairway, his pitch shot finishing 15 feet away. If he misses, I've got two putts for the win, a fact not lost on him. He looks at me and says, 'I suppose I'll have to keep you honest,' which is another way of saying, 'Don't think I'm going to make this easy for you, pal.' He rattles in his birdie putt and, shaken out of my comfort zone, I miss. It's a half rather than the win I'd foolishly envisaged. I sense I've blown my last chance.

I'm dead right about that. One down playing the

last I manage to hook my drive, a couple of firm bounces sending my ball skipping into the long stuff. I hack it out of the hay onto the fairway, while Peter strikes a lovely 4-iron to 15 feet. 'You made the classic mistake on the tee back there,' he says to me as we wander up the fairway. 'You started tight and swung loose. It's what most people do under pressure. When you're nervous, you've got to hold the club softly. Your grip pressure will instinctively become tighter as you hit the ball. It's like cracking a whip: soft to start and then tighter as you apply the "hit".'

Over lunch, Peter jokes that I'll need a calculator to add up his score. In fact he's round in approximately 75 strokes, give or take a few gimmes. Not Open Championship-winning form perhaps, but hardly shabby either.

'I don't play a lot of golf any more, which means I don't play so well,' he says. 'I find myself wasting strokes here and there. But I still enjoy it. I enjoy the fact that I don't have to write the score down, because for 40 years or more that's what I had to do every day. It was a great relief when one day I didn't have to do that!' I ask him if he's ever beaten his age. 'I've never really tried, to be honest. It's so long since I last played a competitive round, but if I played a bit for ten days I'd be beating my age by the end of it.'

Having watched him play, I don't doubt that.

After lunch, we shake hands and go our separate ways. In my job I'm lucky enough to get some wonderful assignments, but by any standards today has been a treat. I have the scorecard and the photos to remind me, but my lasting memory of my game with Peter will be not so much the score he made but the way he played. To Peter Thomson, golf truly is and always has been a simple game. It's the rest of us who make it seem difficult.

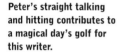

Peter's straight talking and hitting contributes to a magical day's golf for this writer.

PHILLIP PRICE

He sweeps into the car park in a sparkling new silver Porsche, locks it with a flick of his infra-red key and heads towards the hotel, where the door is opened for him by a man in a red jacket. Inside, Celtic Manor's billionaire owner waits to have his picture taken with him, the flash bulbs lighting up a face that bears a relaxed and confident smile.

'There's Wales!'... although you can't see much of it on days like this.

Even on a damp, depressing day when the swirling breeze up the Bristol Channel brings in clouds of misty rain, this man transcends the murky cold. This man is Phillip Price – Ryder Cup player, former journeyman tour pro. What a difference a year can make. Price has been a European tour golfer for close to ten years. He has never rated his chances too highly. A player who has believed himself to be largely inferior to the other golfers around him. A short hitter who says that he was a poor striker of the ball and had to fight tooth and nail just to keep his head above water on tour.

So where is that man now? He is nowhere to be seen when Phillip Price strides into the clubhouse at the appointed time for our match on Celtic Manor's Wentwood Hills Course. The year 2000 was a turnaround year for Phillip. He climbed to fifth on the Ryder Cup points list. He finished in the top ten on the money list with the help of four runner-up spots, amassing more than £750,000 in prize money, sealing his new status with a brilliant performance in the prestigious NEC Invitational where he was beaten only by Tiger Woods. The man is unrecognizable from the one who toiled for so long. As we don our Gore-Tex defences and strap our bags to the back of the buggy, I realize that this remarkable transformation is a mystery I really need to explore.

Splashing through the puddles on our way to the 1st tee, I begin my inquisition. The ensuing conversation makes for a fascinating insight into how a man can change his life around.

But first, let's tee off. Phillip drills a drive down the centre of the opening fairway, delivers an approach that stands smartly to attention on its second bounce, and rolls in the putt for a birdie. I fear this contest might not go the full distance, not only because of my opponent's superiority but because the horrendous conditions are making the game virtually unplayable. We agree by mutual consent that our game should be reduced to a nine-hole affair, taking in the 1st to the 4th and then the 14th to the finish. This will keep us on the higher ground of the Wentwood Hills Course, conveniently out of reach of the two huge lakes which wrap their way around numerous greens in the valley below. I have switched to a two-piece ball in an effort to get a few extra yards – a policy I thought might also have been employed by Phillip. 'No need to.' He grins, holding up a blue-logoed Callaway ball. 'I switched after having a go with it in practice just before the NEC. I borrowed a couple from Stephen Ames and found that I was hitting my drives ten yards further. I've never been a long hitter, so ten yards to me is an awful lot. It means that I can get much closer to the par 5s and

Through hard work and intelligent application Phillip has transformed himself from a struggling tour pro to a Ryder Cup player.

I'm hitting less club into the par 4s. The decision has cost me a bit, because it means I will have to forgo the bonus I was due from Titleist. They told me to play the ball I preferred, so I stuck with the Callaway. I stand to lose around £25,000 because of it.' This switch is one of the reasons Phillip has metamorphosed from workaday tour pro into a player of world-class calibre. As we examine the Callaway Rule 35 ball, he utters a line I'm going to hear twice more this morning. 'It has transformed my game really,' he says.

Although now set fair to become the biggest Welsh talent since Ian Woosnam, Price isn't exactly what you might term 'characteristically Welsh'. He can't sing for a start, refuses to try even a note, even though the only people within earshot are me and the photographer. He loves rugby, but there's a catch. It isn't union, it's league. He hardly misses a Leeds Rhinos match when they're live on television. To top it off, he can't actually speak the language. 'My wife can – she's fluent and she says that when our baby arrives it'll have to learn too,' he says after another monotonously good tee shot down the middle. It transpires that he doesn't much like leeks and he agrees that £4.20 to get into Wales over the Severn Bridge does seem quite a lot. On the other hand, his father's mother's brother was a coal miner, and he admits to owning Tom Jones's latest album.

More important than all this, perhaps, is that this is a man who shunned £25,000 because he preferred one golf ball to another. This, it transpires as we head to the 4th tee, is a clue to another of Phillip's transformations. 'To be successful you sometimes have to make decisions that might be against your natural instincts,' he confides. 'The poor player is the one who employs a cheap local caddie, stays in a cheap hotel, eats fast food because it's cheap and travels on cheap

'THE IDEA IS THAT YOU ALWAYS ACT CONFIDENTLY EVEN IF YOU DON'T FEEL THAT WAY INSIDE. YOU PUFF OUT YOUR CHEST, KEEP YOUR CHIN UP AND MOVE PURPOSEFULLY TO THE BALL.'

flights. If you want to be a class act then you have to behave in the way the best players behave. You stay in the best hotels, you get a good caddie, you dress well and eat well. If you haven't got the guts to do that, then you haven't got the guts to be up there with the best. Look at Lee Westwood and Darren Clarke. They hire private jets and they travel first class. Just doing that makes you feel

PHILLIP ON ...
SQUARING UP TO BUNKERS

In my view, many amateurs hold the clubface too open when they're playing bunker shots. The way the sand-wedge is designed these days means that the bounce on the club is sufficient if you hold it square to the target, especially if you're using a club with, say, 60 degrees of loft. I like to have the club set to aim perhaps a foot right of the pin, and I swing down a line that's probably no more than a foot to the left of it. All this cranking the club wide open and swinging miles across the line is unnecessary unless you're playing some kind of trick shot to a pin just over the lip in front of you.

'IF YOU WANT TO BE A CLASS ACT THEN YOU HAVE TO BEHAVE IN THE WAY THE BEST PLAYERS BEHAVE. YOU STAY IN THE BEST HOTELS, YOU GET A GOOD CADDIE, YOU DRESS WELL AND EAT WELL.'

superior. It makes you feel like you are better than the rest and it helps you to perform in that way too.' That explains Phillip's new Porsche, then. It seems his personal makeover is not so much the result of his recent success as the cause of it.

The inspiration for such positive vibes dates back ten years, to when Price first met the sports psychologist Alan Fine. They have worked together on and off ever since, but in the last few seasons the sessions have really begun to pay off. 'We play a game,' Phillip explains as he tees up his ball, 'and it's called "act as if". The idea is that you always act confidently even if you don't feel that way inside. You puff out your chest, keep your chin

Working with coach Dennis Sheehy has helped him improve his swing, and consequently his ball striking, out of all recognition.

PHILLIP ON ... KEEPING FACE

If you balance your putter on your finger, you'll see that mine is face-balanced – the face points directly to the sky. I prefer this because I feel it helps me to keep the club square through the ball for longer. Conventional putters behave much more like a garden gate, which means they are only aimed perfectly at the target for a fraction of the time as they swing back and through.

PHILLIP ON ... MAINTAINING THE ANGLES

One of the problems I've always had in my swing is a tendency to lift up just as I'm coming into the ball. If you look at Monty and Garcia, they do the opposite – they go down a little as they hit the ball. For me, it's a question of maintaining my spine angle through the shot, and this is something I have worked hard on with Dennis Sheehy. Lifting up means that I get too flippy with my hands through the ball and I hook it. That's why it's noticeable that I keep my spine angle tilted over the ball for longer than other players before moving into the finish position of my swing. I have to concentrate on maintaining my address posture, and keeping my backside sticking out. On a poor shot my backside comes in and my spine angle becomes more vertical. This is also why I tee the ball low with my driver. I used to have it much higher, but I found that it only encouraged me to lift up when I hit it.

up and move purposefully to the ball. You have a confident look on your face. I do it a lot with my face. Sometimes it helps if I think of certain players. For example, when I'm chipping I sometimes think I'm Seve Ballesteros. This is an attitude that you should maintain as much as you can, and I don't just mean on the golf course.'

We hop back into the buggy and head up the cart path. I'm intrigued to know more about this play-acting, so I ask Phillip to explain some more. 'I've decided that you get what you expect out of life,' he replies. 'Not what you hope for, but what you expect. It's as I said – if you want to be a top player then you must run your life accordingly. I fly club class now, not economy.'

But don't you have any doubts about all of this?

'Oh yes. You think, "Am I doing the right thing?" I question it a lot. Is this a waste of money? Is it really going to make a difference? But I've had a lot of evidence to say that it does, it makes the world of difference.'

The subject of psychology is one I'm keen to pursue further, so I ask Phillip what his expectations were when he first met up with Alan Fine. 'I was so far off track,' he admits. 'I lacked confidence in myself as a person, as much as anything else. I never thought I'd ever be able to make money playing golf. I didn't think I'd ever be able to play on the tour. I just didn't think I was

Phillip has had to work hard on staying down through the hitting area, but there's still some room for improvement.

good enough. I didn't think I was very good at anything, to be honest.'

It's strange listening to him, as if the weak man is still in there somewhere, locked in some dungeon in his psyche. You can't help but feel a little sympathy for the little chap left behind.

'So what's your expectation now?' I ask him. 'You've gone from having a big inferiority complex to what, exactly?'

'My expectation now is far greater. I'm looking to win the events I play in. I'm expecting to get into the Ryder Cup side next year [he did]. I know I'm good enough, there's no doubt about that.'

'And majors?'

'That's the next level. I haven't played in many majors and I haven't played against the best all that often. I'm looking forward to getting that sort of experience.'

And that's not all. Phillip's horizons have risen so sharply that already he's casting glances across the Atlantic. 'I'll concentrate on the Ryder Cup, but at the end of the season I'll look to the qualifying school over there. Playing the few tournaments I have in America has been terrific experience, and I feel like I owe it to myself to give it a try over there. I'd like to see how well I can play at the top level.'

Just as we are about to discuss another transformation, a par from Phillip closes me out

'THAT'S THE NEXT LEVEL. I HAVEN'T PLAYED IN MANY MAJORS AND I HAVEN'T PLAYED AGAINST THE BEST ALL THAT OFTEN. I'M LOOKING FORWARD TO GETTING THAT SORT OF EXPERIENCE.'

and the match is over. We steer the buggy towards the comfort of the clubhouse.

'Another thing that transformed my game was changing my coach at the end of last year,' Phillip says as we trundle up the path. 'Dennis Sheehy has really got to take a tremendous amount of credit. I've noticed a massive difference in my ball striking.

I hit the ball reasonably now – not like the best, but pretty good – whereas before I was one of the worst hitters on tour. Bad technique, bad hitter.'

Price has been quite alarmingly honest throughout our round, which I suppose is easier to do when you've solved your most pressing problems. Even so, a morning in the company of Phillip Price has turned out to be both an entertaining and eye-opening experience. When he's not imagining he's Seve Ballesteros, he remains quite a shy man, but that trait should not be confused with being dull and uninteresting. When it comes to strength of character Phillip Price takes some beating, especially now that he has found something he's good at. Very good, actually.

RETIEF GOOSEN

Retief Goosen was struck by lightning as a youngster. Some of the electricity became permanently lodged in his brain, and now helps him to generate enormous power from the most effortless of golf swings.

Retief punches a wedge shot down the hill on this pretty little par-3 at Woburn.

Okay, so only the first of those two sentences is scientific fact. But nothing would surprise me, because there is something other-worldly about the way this softly spoken South African hammers a golf ball. I'd encountered Retief once before, but it's still a major eye-opener to stand next to him as he unleashes his first tee shot of the day.

We are playing together in a pro am at Woburn. Retief is a picture of health, a walking, talking testament to the benefits of an outdoor life – in marked contrast to his three pasty-faced, office-bound playing partners. He's a whisker under six feet tall, but seems bigger because of his powerful build. But he's not intimidating. He has an almost gentle way about him. Not the type to get easily rattled. Sometimes this unassuming nature gets abused, even by pro am partners. 'Last year I was paired with a guy who kept

telling me to stand still or move to one side,' he tells me, still incredulous about it. 'I couldn't believe it.'

That day Retief kept shtum and let his game do the talking. Any sensible amateur would do best simply to shut up, watch and learn. Over our early holes there is plenty to admire, and it's easy to see why his career earnings nudge £4 million and he has 13 pro victories to his name, the most prized of those being the 2001 US Open. In team golf he has twice been a winner for South Africa in the Dunhill Cup, once chalking up ten straight match wins – just one shy of Greg Norman's all-time record.

'I USED TO SWING FLAT OUT ALL THE TIME, BUT NOW I WOULD SAY I SWING AT ABOUT 80 PER CENT. THAT HAS HELPED MY BALANCE AND IMPROVED MY CONSISTENCY.'

There was a time when he might have felt a slight twinge of untapped potential. But working with Belgian sports psychologist Jos Vanstiphout, who counsels several leading players on the tour, taught him to believe in himself more. 'It's helped, because I always felt I had a bit of a temperament problem and recently that's improved a lot,' Retief explains. 'Mentally I feel like I'm on more of an even keel. I used to get a bit down if I wasn't playing well and I'd tend to drag a bad hole on for too long rather than forgetting about it. My self-confidence is better, too.'

This new-found attitude, combined with his naturally calm personality, stood him in good stead on his way to bagging his first major. Needing to two-putt from 12 feet on the final green for victory, he inexplicably three-putted to send the tournament into a play-off the following

RETIEF ON ...
SWINGING WITH RHYTHM

I don't think my swing is so bad that I need to work on too many things. I like to give myself room at address, so my hands are well away from the tops of my thighs. This encourages a wider extension in the takeaway, my hands and the club moving away more in one piece. It also gives me room to get a better release and extension through the ball. If you're too close to the ball at address you never have the room to do that; you end up too cramped at impact and unable to swing the club freely through the ball. That costs you power. Otherwise, I just try to work on good rhythm and timing. I concentrate on making a nice, smooth swing. I generate plenty of power but I don't try to hit the ball too hard — I feel like it's a controlled hit. I used to swing flat out all the time, but now I would say I swing at about 80 per cent. That has helped my balance and improved my consistency. I think most amateurs would benefit if they focused a bit more on their rhythm and timing.

Retief doesn't hit too many tee shots off line, but when he does his recovery play is more than up to the challenge.

day with Mark Brooks. That Retief was able to take this blow on the chin and play so well the following day to take the title speaks volumes for the quality of his grey matter.

'Walking off the 72nd green,' he recalls, 'I was honestly fine about what had happened. Everybody else seemed to be devastated though. When I was walking back to the clubhouse everybody I saw had red eyes and I was thinking, "Who's funeral are we at?" I sat down and I just looked at it as a learning experience, not as a disaster. Obviously it's not how you'd choose for things to happen, but you learn from it, you try not to let it upset you too much and hopefully you become a better player because of it. On the Sunday night I had a chat with Jos and he asked me how I felt. I told him I felt good. I hadn't played badly, I'd played well, so there was nothing to blame myself for. I deserved to be where I was. That was the thing in my mind, I hadn't lost the tournament. I knew I was going to wake up the next morning and have a chance to win the US Open.'

As is often the case with golfers, Retief's game reflects his personality: quiet, unhurried, but all things executed with great purpose. He sets up to the ball in a relaxed, methodical fashion. His hold on the club is soft, but his huge tanned forearms give the promise of a powerful thump to come. Sometimes as he stands over the ball he subtly lifts his chin up, as if to remind himself to make way for the massive shoulder turn that is such a key feature of his golf swing. His first move away from the ball is very correct, very smooth. The

RETIEF ON ...
BUNKER PLAY MADE EASY

I carry two wedges that I can use in bunkers, a lob-wedge and a normal sand-wedge. Which I use depends on how far I want to hit it and how quickly I want to stop it. But once I've made up my mind, the actual technique changes very little from shot to shot. I vary the amount I open the blade depending on how far I want to hit it, but other than varying the length of swing everything else stays much the same. I use quite a quick wrist-break at the start of the swing. I don't look at the ball, but at the point in the sand behind the ball where I want the clubhead to come down. Then I just try to hit that spot and follow through.

club doesn't quite reach horizontal at the top, and just as he gets there he switches from deliberate to dynamic as the lower half goes into overdrive. His hips clear out of the way very quickly – not quite Tiger-speed, but pretty rapid nonetheless. The hands, arms and club then just seem to drop into the ideal slot, and he rips through the ball.

The sound of the club striking home is alarmingly loud, as if he were playing with one of those rock-like ultra-distance balls. Except that he's not. Retief's golf ball has a relatively soft cover and is constructed with maximum control in mind. It's a 1.68-inch guided missile. He hits some shots that draw gasps and murmurs from the small gallery, which then turn into applause. On the par-5 10th, he hits what I genuinely feel is one of the most impressive shots I've ever seen, not because the circumstances are extraordinary but because the ball-flight is just so downright jaw-droppingly awesome.

Retief has 194 yards to the pin, with the ball resting on a downslope in the left side of the fairway. Hidden from view is a bunker protecting today's pin position. He makes his customary unhurried backswing, then surges into his downswing to produce the unmistakable sound of a cleanly struck iron shot.

'Smooth acceleration gives you more speed,' he says simply.

For the first 50 yards of its journey the ball gets barely 8 feet above ground. Then, from this most pure and powerful of hits, it suddenly acquires the gift of lift and soars upwards and onwards. It eventually comes down exactly 190 yards away, dropping from a height of about 40 feet and landing as softly as a sparrow wearing slippers. Retief holes the eight-foot putt for an eagle three, which is nothing less than his second shot deserved. I remark on what a phenomenal shot it was, and with a hint of a smile he just says, 'It was a slight hanging lie, which helped the trajectory.' Master of the understatement, is Retief.

However, as the round continues I feel there's a hint of Monty in Retief's game, in the sense that a lot of tremendous shots seem to go unrewarded on the greens. Later, back in the office, I find my suspicions are supported by his performance stats on tour. He doesn't excel in any single department, but his putting is markedly poorer than the rest of his game. Retief averages nearly 31 putts per round, which is nearly 3 putts per round worse than the leading putter on tour. It

ties him 140th in the putting rankings – a lowly position given his standing in the game.

With someone like Retief, it's hard to put your finger on exactly why he doesn't make more putts. The stroke looks sound and the ball frequently seems to threaten the hole. But then I've often wondered about the magic ingredient that enables some golfers to hole putts from all over the place, while others seem always to be shaving the hole.

A human being surely can't influence by fractions of an inch the final destination of a ball running 30, 40, 50 or even 60 feet across an imperfect playing surface. You can make the perfect read, produce the perfect stroke, but I suspect the final outcome is not in the hands of the player, rather those of Lady Luck. If so, Retief is not the luckiest bloke in the world – although saying that he's twice shot 62, one of them the current course record at Loch Lomond. A flick through the player profiles in the European Tour handbook reveals that not many pros ever shoot that low in their careers.

Back to today's game, though. I'm no veteran of the pro am scene, but aside from the odd wasted stroke (some of them very odd indeed) from we three amateurs, our fourball seems to be doing quite nicely. With only one score counting from four, we reach the turn seven strokes under par, and begin to speculate about what might be a winning number. Suddenly Retief interjects: 'Maybe 18 under.' Oh dear.

Never mind. On the 13th, a big par 5, our pro's effortless power is again on full display. With 280 yards to the front edge, he stands over his second

Softly-spoken and charming, the 2001 US Open champion is the perfect playing companion.

'MENTALLY I FEEL LIKE I'M ON MORE OF AN EVEN KEEL. I USED TO GET A BIT DOWN IF I WASN'T PLAYING WELL AND I'D TEND TO DRAG A BAD HOLE ON FOR TOO LONG . . . '

shot, eyeing the green and wondering whether or not to wait for it to clear. With the flag on the top tier 30 yards back and all four members of the group occupying that portion of the green, he eventually decides it is safe to go. They are, after all, more than 300 yards away.

He takes out his driver, and after a swing of sublime rhythm the ball explodes off the clubface. The flight is implausibly high considering the ball was struck off a closely mown fairway, and it actually pitches on the front edge. It rolls diagonally up the step in the green but just lacks the momentum to make it to the top and trundles backwards down the slope.

'I didn't think I was going to get there,' he says, adding, with more than a smidgen of modesty, 'But I hit it pretty good.'

No kidding!

Retief waves an apology to the group in front, although tour pro Sven Struver is not in the least perturbed. Bizarrely, it turns out that one of his amateur partners is slightly miffed about the episode, which is pathetic. I mean, nobody was in danger. As far as I know there is no record of a trundling golf ball causing life-threatening injuries. The guy perhaps would have done better merely to marvel at Retief's awesome shot. He might have learned something.

I know I'm learning plenty, and my playing partners express similar sentiments. As far as our score goes, however, there are rather too many problems and too little time to solve them all. Despite a very solid performance from Retief, who I'd guess finishes about four under par, the 18th comes a few holes too soon. As it turns out, a 16-under-par 56 wins the pro am, which puts our 59 in the shade. Still, it's good enough for a top-three finish, and we take home some rather handsome whisky tumblers. Not to mention some vivid memories of precisely how a golf ball should be hit.

Retief keeps his technique in the sand basically the same for every shot, simply altering the length of his swing to send the ball different distances through the air.

RETIEF ON ... PLAYING THE 'PUTT CHIP'

This is the way I tend to play most of my chip shots, unless the situation prevents me from doing so – if I have to fly a bunker, for example. It's like an extended putting stroke really. I play it with a conventional grip, a narrow stance, the ball back and my hands leading. It's important to concentrate on keeping the left wrist square going through to the hole, so you don't scoop at the ball or catch it fat. My aim is always to carry the ball just onto the green and let it run to the hole from there, so I select whatever club does that job. As a rule, the less green I have to work with, the more loft I use. I think this is where some amateurs waste a lot of shots. The first mistake they make is automatically choosing a wedge. That club generates lots of height and spin, which makes it very easy to leave the ball short of the hole. If you go with less loft, with the 7-iron I'm using here for instance, it's so much easier to get the ball within holing-out range. You need to hit a few practice shots to get the hang of it, but soon you'll find the 'putt chip' is by far the best method for getting up and down with minimum fuss.

TONY JACKLIN

He is one of Britain's all-time sporting heroes, the man who made the Ryder Cup the biggest event in golf. As I amble up to Tony Jacklin on the putting green at Kungsangen GC near Stockholm, I can't help noticing his relaxed demeanour. On the eve of the STC Scandinavian International, one of his rare outings on the European Seniors Tour, Jacko seems comfortable with his lot in life as a gently ageing legend of British sport. Even his cream, chunky-knit, short-sleeved cardigan and greying temples give him an air of the father figure of British golf.

Head-to-head with a Ryder Cup legend, captain Tony Jacklin, the man who helped revive Europe's fortunes.

The stresses of tournament golf are a distant memory for Jacklin and he now seems totally content with his life.

While I know that Tony's golf is far from the bristling game it was when he became a double major champion, it's still daunting to face a man who trailblazed for his country in the late 1960s and early 1970s. Not only was he the sole Brit to win the Open Championship between Max Faulkner in 1951 and Sandy Lyle in 1985, he's still the only European US Open champion since Ted Ray in 1920. He belongs in the pantheon of great sporting Britons alongside Denis Compton, Stanley Matthews, Fred Perry and Steve Redgrave.

So you might expect Tony Jacklin to be threatening or aloof, but as we set off down the 1st in a blustery wind he seems almost oblivious to his standing within the game. It's not until the 3rd that we start to chat about the Ryder Cup. Although 1967 was the first time he played in the matches, 1957 – the year Great Britain & Ireland sneaked past the United States at Lindrick – was Jacko's Ryder Cup baptism. As a 12-handicap 13-year-old his father took him from their home in Scunthorpe to watch the tussle. 'I remember touching Dai Rees's driver walking down the fairway, and he asked me to put a divot back. Ten years later he was my captain at the Champions' Club in Texas. It was a strange turnaround.'

When Tony rolls in a birdie putt from 12 feet for a win at the 3rd, I begin to see what all the fuss was about those 30 years ago. With a twitchy breeze buffeting us on the short 4th, he strikes a pure 5-iron, the clubhead barely grazing the turf, and the ball finishes within a couple of paces. He then sinks the slick left-to-righter without a hint of the anxiety that made him give up full-time golf in the 1980s. He confesses to his flaw after going two up: 'I stopped when I was 40 because I got so anxious on the greens. I played from tee to green great but at times putted like a fool. It wasn't because I was a bad putter, just that I was so nervous. I just didn't enjoy it.'

With the pressure off, Tony again looks like a man capable of stringing a few birdies together. As we walk to the elevated tee at Kungsangen's 6th, a downhill par 3 over water, I ask him about how the emergence of the European team coincided with his

reign of captaincy. I suggest that he catalysed the upturn in European fortunes. He's embarrassed enough to be put off his stroke, flies the green with a 7-iron, then talks about the problems before the golden years. 'Back in the 1950s and 1960s there was a lot of bravado coming from the Great Britain & Ireland team, because I'm convinced they were in awe of the likes of Ben Hogan and Sam Snead. And because of my experience playing in the US, I thought I knew what had to be done. What inspired us was the feeling that the Americans had it all. We wanted to show that given a level playing field we had a chance. That's what I wanted to achieve as captain, to get the off-course things right – caddies travelling with us, creating a team room and so on. Getting those things right coincided with the arrival of the Seves, Faldos, Langers and Lyles on the course. It was perfect timing.'

Tony takes me back to the 1983 match at PGA National in Florida. 'The press gave us no credence at all. Most went off to Disney World and came back with Mickey Mouse bags. Yet it looked like we were going to win all day Sunday, until Lanny Wadkins hit that wedge at 18. But there was wonderful camaraderie. We could sense that things were gelling. It was a fantastic effort, and a stepping stone. In 1985 we talked about going close

HE BELONGS IN THE PANTHEON OF GREAT SPORTING BRITONS ALONGSIDE DENIS COMPTON, STANLEY MATTHEWS, FRED PERRY AND STEVE REDGRAVE

last time. We sensed, given home advantage, that we could win.'

Such is Tony's passion for the Ryder Cup, and fascination with its history, that he has even commissioned a set of limited edition Ryder Cup furniture, some of it crafted by Lord Linley, its centrepiece a reproduction of Sam Ryder's old desk, which he bought to use himself in 1989.

I put his slightly wayward approach shot at the 7th down to the waves of nostalgia washing over him, and manage to capitalize with a surprising birdie. I come quickly back down to earth at the 8th, however, when I flounder among the granite outcrops and the match returns to parity. Just as my run reaches an abrupt end, one of a different kind starts for Tony as he sprints towards the nearest portaloo. Even at the age of 57, he shows the fleetness of foot of a desperate man.

A few minutes later he trots back, and his new-found freedom of swing nails one down the par 5. I watch his action intently. With a squat but rock-solid stance, he is one of the old school as he turns and thumps. It is his hand-eye coordination mixed with bricklayer's forearms and cyclist's thighs that power the ball away. No frills, no nonsense. Just natural ability rolled into a mighty meatball. He comfortably reaches the 513-yard hole in two

Young 'Jacko' watches his dad in action.

JACKO ON ...
WHAT MAKES A GOOD CAPTAIN

You have to be passionate about it. I put a lot of energy and thought in, and tried not to leave any stone unturned in terms of detail. With the pairings, I always tried to have the courage to do what I felt in my heart was the right thing. Sometimes you might get notions, and you must back those hunches. The worst thing to do is to walk into the team room and open it up to the floor. Sure, I bounced ideas off Seve, my man on the course, but ultimately it's the captain's decision. I think the cup is in good hands in Sam and Curtis. They have both had the pleasure and the pain of winning and losing, and know what it's all about.

There's a freedom of movement in Tony's swing that harks back to his heyday and he gives the ball a solid thump with those strong, bricklayer's forearms.

JACKO ON ...
THE NICKLAUS
CONCESSION IN 1969

It was two feet – not three or four, as some have said, but two. Was I pleased that he gave it to me? Relieved would be a better word! Could it happen today? I think yes. Jack and I were friends, our wives were friends, we fished together, we were pals. I was one of the few to go to America and play, but now many do, so friendships have been struck. I will tell you, though, that while it was a sporting gesture between friends, some of the Americans weren't so happy. There were some mean-spirited guys on that team in 1969. Sam Snead was captain then, and he is a hard man. It didn't go down as well with Jack's team-mates as it did with everyone else.

'I STOPPED WHEN I WAS 40 BECAUSE I GOT SO ANXIOUS ON THE GREENS. I PLAYED FROM TEE TO GREEN GREAT BUT AT TIMES PUTTED LIKE A FOOL.'

eagle, thought I'd won my match, but they didn't know I had lost 16. You don't want to be where Jack and I were that day. I walked down the hill on 18 having hit a 3-wood, and he hollered at me, "Tony, are you nervous?" I said, "Nervous? I'm petrified." And he replied, "I thought I'd ask, because if it's any consolation I feel exactly the same as you do."'

The valve was loosened and the streams of relief burst out when Jack conceded 'that putt' for a half and a tie.

Before we take on our 18th, a brute of 426 yards uphill and into the wind, Tony's charming nine-year-old son Sean shows us how the Jacklin legend may live on. Barely bigger than the bag he has been pulling for 17 holes, Sean stands up on the tee with his dad's driver and swings majestically at the ball, which rockets away to just shy of the 200-yard mark. We laugh. What price a Jacklin playing at Medinah in the 2011 Ryder Cup? 'He's got it all this kid, I tell you,' coos Dad.

But this hole more than any other today proves to me what talent still lurks beneath Jacklin Senior's fatherly exterior. A rasping drive down the middle is followed by a world-class 3-iron that, if transplanted to the wilds of a links, would have the galleries in raptures. All that's left is for Tony to coax his first putt to the brink of the hole. And although the second putt is truly unmissable, I can't help but pick it up and concede the halved match à la Nicklaus.

Tony puts our day and the forthcoming Ryder Cup into perspective. 'As long as it's a great contest conducted by gentlemen, where on the 1st tee you look your opponent in the eye and keep the game as sportsmanlike as possible, it doesn't matter who wins.' Amen to that.

I've enjoyed Jacko's company greatly. Although some have found him a little too outspoken and self-congratulatory at times, I find him nothing but one of those 'gentlemen' he referred to. He is honest, and any slight immodesty is born from a genuine boyish pleasure about what he has achieved in the game. And let's face it, Tony Jacklin has much to shout about. We should be grateful for his achievements and his amazing input into the success of the Ryder Cup.

but zooms through the back.

As he pops another delightful lob at the 11th – his secret is to keep his left hand and clubface going through together – Tony talks about the wonders of team golf. 'Individual wins are purely selfish pursuits, but there are so many people involved with a Ryder Cup that winning one is very special. Don't get me wrong, I felt marvellous after my Open wins, but the Ryder Cup is somehow beyond that. The last thing I said before I left as captain was, "Whatever you do, don't change the format." To me it's a great format that probably favours the underdog, because you are not showing all your cards before Sunday. That almost guarantees a close contest.'

In 1971, Jacklin was turned over at the last in the final morning's singles by motormouth Lee Trevino, and inadvertently my Ryder Cup inquisition seems to break Tony's concentration enough for me to sneak one ahead with one to play. To me this is a pressure moment, but not in the least bit to Tony. He has experienced one of the most extreme situations ever seen in golf. In 1969, he and Jack Nicklaus were the last singles out on the course with the outcome of the Ryder Cup hingeing on their game. Jacklin had just lost 16 to go one down, and the tension was furious.

'The pressure was enormous, because you put yourself last,' he recalls. 'The team comes first. I knew the score better than anyone else. Everyone on 18 who heard the roar from 17, where I'd holed for

The thrill of competition wore off for Tony in the early-80s. While still striking the ball well, his putting became a source of frustration.

**JACKO'S RYDER CUP
RECORD AS A CAPTAIN**

PLAYED 4, WON 2, HALVED 1, LOST 1
POINTS: EUROPE 59   USA 53

**JACKO'S RYDER CUP
RECORD AS A PLAYER**

PLAYED 35, WON 13, HALVED 8, LOST 14

INDEX